Editor-in-Chief and Founder:
  Lyndon H. LaRouche, Jr.
Editorial Board: *Lyndon H. LaRouche, Jr. , Helga
  Zepp-LaRouche, Robert Ingraham, Tony
  Papert, Gerald Rose, Dennis Small, Jeffrey
  Steinberg, William Wertz*
Co-Editors: *Robert Ingraham, Tony Papert*
Managing Editor: *Nancy Spannaus*
Technology: *Marsha Freeman*
Books: *Katherine Notley*
Ebooks: *Richard Burden*
Graphics: *Alan Yue*
Photos: *Stuart Lewis*
Circulation Manager: *Stanley Ezrol*

INTELLIGENCE DIRECTORS
Counterintelligence: *Jeffrey Steinberg, Michele
  Steinberg*
Economics: *John Hoefle, Marcia Merry Baker,
  Paul Gallagher*
History: *Anton Chaitkin*
Ibero-America: *Dennis Small*
Russia and Eastern Europe: *Rachel Douglas*
United States: *Debra Freeman*

INTERNATIONAL BUREAUS
Bogotá: *Miriam Redondo*
Berlin: *Rainer Apel*
Copenhagen: *Tom Gillesberg*
Houston: *Harley Schlanger*
Lima: *Sara Madueño*
Melbourne: *Robert Barwick*
Mexico City: *Gerardo Castilleja Chávez*
New Delhi: *Ramtanu Maitra*
Paris: *Christine Bierre*
Stockholm: *Ulf Sandmark*
United Nations, N.Y.C.: *Leni Rubinstein*
Washington, D.C.: *William Jones*
Wiesbaden: *Göran Haglund*

ON THE WEB
e-mail: eirns@larouchepub.com
www.larouchepub.com
www.executiveintelligencereview.com
www.larouchepub.com/eiw
Webmaster: *John Sigerson*
Assistant Webmaster: *George Hollis*
Editor, Arabic-language edition: *Hussein Askary*

EIR (ISSN 0273-6314) *is published weekly
(50 issues), by EIR News Service, Inc.,
P.O. Box 17390, Washington, D.C. 20041-0390.
(703) 777-9451 ext. 415*

European Headquarters: E.I.R. GmbH, Postfach
Bahnstrasse 9a, D-65205, Wiesbaden, Germany
Tel: 49-611-73650
Homepage: http://www.eirna.com
e-mail: eirna@eirna.com
Director: Georg Neudecker

Montreal, Canada: 514-461-1557

Denmark: EIR - Danmark, Sankt Knuds Vej 11,
basement left, DK-1903 Frederiksberg, Denmark.
Tel.: +45 35 43 60 40, Fax: +45 35 43 87 57. e-mail:
eirdk@hotmail.com.

Mexico City: EIR, Sor Juana Inés de la Cruz 242-2
Col. Agricultura C.P. 11360
Delegación M. Hidalgo, México D.F.
Tel. (5525) 5318-2301
eirmexico@gmail.com

Canada Post Publication Sales Agreement
#40683579

Postmaster: Send all address changes to *EIR*, P.O.
Box 17390, Washington, D.C. 20041-0390.

Signed articles in *EIR* represent the views of the
authors, and not necessarily those of the Editorial
Board.

Productivity

Revolt of the Lame Ducks in Berlin: The Music of History Plays Elsewhere

by Helga Zepp-LaRouche, chairwoman of the German political party Civil Rights Movement Solidarity (BüSo)

Nov. 19—The great waves of hysteria in die-hard Atlanticist circles and the mass media, which were already sweeping in before the U.S. election, have reached an unprecedented scale since Trump's victory, and give us clinical insight into the mental state and understanding of democracy of these people. Evidently they would rather have a President Hillary Clinton and a Third World War resulting from her announced Syria policy, than the potential improvement of Russian-American relations, which is indispensable for establishing world peace and achieving positive solutions for Syria and Ukraine.

It is truly remarkable: After the repudiated President Obama managed to find three days to stay at Berlin's Hotel Adlon, and to dine and talk with his friend Angela Merkel, and then to hold a mini-summit of the self-appointed European "Six," the two of them decided—along with the other heads of state—to prolong the sanctions against Russia for another year. These not-so-secure others were French President François Hollande (7% approval rating), Italian Prime Minister Matteo Renzi (the likely loser in an Italian referendum on Dec. 4), Spanish Prime Minister Mariano Rajoy (interim head of state of a minority government), and the hapless British Prime Minister Theresa May. It is doubtful that they will contribute to cohesion in the EU with this move to make themselves a virtual Directorate of the European Union, and then decree a policy which half of the EU member countries oppose.

Our Inalienable Rights

This self-anointed "Six" have obviously not yet grasped that their variant of neoliberal policy, based on confrontation with Russia and China, was voted out in the Brexit vote in June and in the recent presidential election in the United States.

They have not understood that a situation has developed in the trans-Atlantic world that is evoked in the American Declaration of Independence: namely, that if governments have become "destructive" "of the ends" of their mandate—specifically, to guarantee the inalienable rights to life, liberty, and the pursuit of happiness—then it is the right of the people, indeed it is their "their duty" to alter or abolish such a government. The "long train of abuses and usurpations" elaborated in the Declaration of Independence corresponds exactly to what those people whom Hillary Clinton so contemptuously called the "basket of deplorables" have endured under Obama's policies—abuses and usurpations which they did not want continued under a President Hillary Clinton.

The self-anointed Six, and above all, the utterly crazed members of the media, who themselves do not shrink from issuing threats against Trump, disguised as humor, are so imprisoned in their own ideology that they cannot grasp the natural-law dimension of this revolution.

Yet the *New York Times* on Nov. 18 published an article on its front page with the headline "Trump-Size Idea for a New President: Build Something Inspiring." The *Times* stated correctly that Trump can only unite the country if he brings on line investments in great infrastructure projects, the likes of which have been totally ignored over the last decades. He must build modern versions of Franklin D. Roosevelt's Golden Gate Bridge, Hoover Dam, and Lincoln Tunnel. Then the "newspaper of record" enumerated Roosevelt's most important projects. But the article is, of course, far behind the program of Lyndon LaRouche, who in 2015 published a proposal to build the New Silk Road in the United States—a program of large-scale infrastructure building and reindustrialization—which would integrate the United States into the World Land-Bridge.

The APEC Summit

Meanwhile, the "win-win cooperation" for development of the New Silk Road is going forward in giant steps. It is *the* dominant theme at the Asia-Pacific Economic Cooperation (APEC) summit in Lima, the Peruvian capital, on Nov. 19-20, in which Chinese President Xi Jinping and Russian President Vladimir Putin, as well as Japanese Prime Minister Shinzo Abe, are participating and at which they are also holding bilateral meetings. Abe had met with President-elect Trump beforehand, and attested to his admirable leadership qualities.

President Xi paid a state visit to Ecuador prior to the APEC summit and has state visits scheduled in Peru and Chile afterwards. President Xi and Ecuador's President Rafael Correa agreed on a "Comprehensive Strategic Partnership" between their two nations, which involves regular, wide-ranging exchange and cooperation on a broad range of issues. Among them are strengthened productive investment, the development of economic and trade relations, economic cooperation, and cooperation in science and technology. China has already provided generous aid for the reconstruction of buildings and grounds which were destroyed in the severe earthquake in April of this year.

President Correa gave eloquent thanks to China in which he stressed that the two countries were of a like mind. China wants to place its economy on the foundation of innovation; Ecuador seeks to progress from being an exporter of goods to being a knowledge-based economy. Without Chinese financing and technology transfer, it would be impossible. In a joint declaration, they pledged to work together for the realization of great projects in the areas of oil, gas, mining, infrastructure, water, water management, communications, the financial sector, agriculture, petrochemical production, shipbuilding, metallurgy, paper production, and the construction of a new science city. In his speech, President Correa stressed that President Xi's state visit was the most important event in the history of Ecuador.

Can you imagine Chancellor Merkel going to Greece with such a program? Probably not. Finance Minister Wolfgang Schäuble turns red when a journalist asks about partial debt relief—as he did at a bankers' conference in Frankfurt—and then pontificates about the Greeks having lived beyond their means. This, after the Troika's austerity policy has driven 45 percent of Greeks below the poverty line. The policy of the trans-Atlantic sector is not "win-win," but "lose-lose"—unless, of course, one is a banker or a corporate executive.

The Interests of *One* Mankind

Now that Obama's free trade deal for Asia, the TPP, is now as dead as the TTIP deal for the Atlantic region, it is the Chinese-designed, inclusive Free Trade Area of the Asia-Pacific (FTAAP) and the Regional Comprehensive Partnership (RCEP) that are on the agenda.

In answer to irresponsible media articles about these trade agreements, official Russian and Chinese spokesmen stressed that they are in no way intended to shut out or isolate the United States. Xinhua quoted Chinese Foreign Ministry spokesman Geng Shuang saying that China would not seize a leading role in either the FTAAP or the RCEP, and that the trade agreements are proposed for working together, not against one another. The contrast with Obama's "the United States makes the rules" could not be clearer.

Another important subject of discussion at the APEC conference is the construction of the bioceanic railroad from Brazil to Peru, from the Atlantic to the Pacific, which will also be built with China's help, and whose construction is an important step toward the infrastructural development of the Latin American continent.

The contrast between the two paradigms, between the "win-win perspective" of the New Silk Road, versus the "Western community of values" of Obama and Merkel, could not be more obvious. In the first, nations work for the mutual advantage of their common development. In the latter, there is much talk of democracy, freedom, and human rights, but a deafening silence on drone strikes, regime change against legitimate governments with the aid of terrorist groups, total surveillance, and life-shortening austerity policies.

As Abraham Lincoln once said: "You can fool some of the people all of the time, and all of the people some of the time. But you can't fool all of the people all of the time."

It is high time that Germany freed itself from the grip of the fantasy of imperial dominance, be it dictated from Washington and London, or the derivative of "More Europe." Mankind's future can only lie in a completely new paradigm that serves the interests of *one* mankind and respects international law—a paradigm through which the creative potential of every human being on this planet can be developed. And that is exactly why we need to cooperate with the New Silk Road.

Written for the newspaper Neue Solidarität *and translated from German.*

EIRContents

www.larouchepub.com Volume 43, Number 48, November 25, 2016

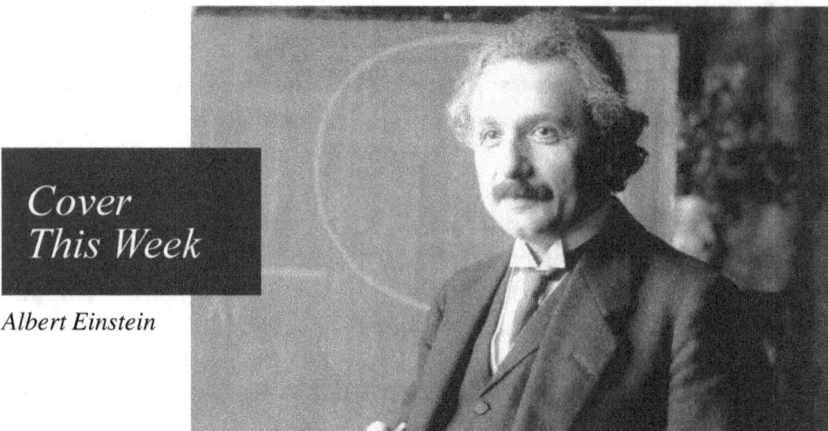

I. The New World System

HELGA ZEPP-LAROUCHE ADDRESSES PERU ASSOCIATION OF ECONOMISTS

The New Silk Road Concept, Facing the Collapse of the World Financial System

On November 17, Schiller Institute founder Helga Zepp-LaRouche delivered the following keynote address to the XXIII National Congress of the Association of Economists of Peru, held in Pucallpa, Ucayali, in the Amazon region of Peru. The title of the Nov. 17-19 congress is "The Peru-Brazil Bi-Oceanic Train: Impact on the Economy of the Amazon Region and the Country." Zepp-LaRouche's presentation, delivered at the opening session on Nov. 17, was on "The New Silk Road Concept, Facing the Collapse of the World Financial System." The Peruvian economists' congress was timed to coincide with the

Helga Zepp-LaRouche

Nov. 19-20 APEC summit in Lima, Peru, with the expected participation of numerous heads of state, including China's Xi Jinping and Russia's Vladimir Putin.

Dear ladies and gentlemen, honorable guests of this very important conference: I am extremely honored to be able to speak to you. This conference is very important, not only for Peru and the rest of Latin America, because it deals not just with infrastructure and rail lines, but because it is really about a paradigm shift to a completely new economic system which is eminently possible to realize. Now, obviously, the context of everything has changed with the unexpected, or for some

unexpected, outcome of the American election. It was not just that people voted for Trump, but that they voted against the war policy of Hillary Clinton, which they perceived as the continuation of the present confrontation of the Obama Administration towards Russia and to a certain extent against China. And they also voted against the absolute injustice of a system which has increased the gap between rich and poor to an unbearable degree.

Now, if you look at what caused the actual election result, it was the voters in the so-called "rust belt" in the formerly industrialized states of Ohio, Wisconsin, and Pennsylvania, people who lost employment, who became impoverished, who had no future, and they just gave an absolute repudiation of these policies.

It is an open secret that the U.S. economy is in a much worse state than the official statistics would try to have you believe. As a matter of fact, in certain European economic circles, they call the United States "the country of the limitless statistical possibilities," meaning that these statistics are all massaged and are a paper tiger. And as people know, you can't eat a paper tiger, you can't fill a hungry stomach with that.

The revolt of the population took a first, very, very dramatic expression in June with the Brexit, the announced exit of Great Britain from the European Union. I would say that the Trump victory in the United States is a reflection of this same rejection of the policy of the establishment, where people feel that this establishment has completely gotten out of synch with the interests of the common people. Therefore, unless the policies are dramatically changed, in all of the United States and in all of Europe, and many other parts of the world, one has to expect more such populist revolts, such rejections of existing policies.

In his acceptance speech, where Trump all of a sudden was more statesmanlike, he not only promised that he would be the President for all Americans, but he announced that he would rebuild the United States economy: Build roads, bridges, train systems, and he even said that he would make the United States the most modern infrastructure in a few years, which is a big promise, given the infrastructure development in other parts of the world already. But he promised that he would reconstruct the real economy of the United States.

Cabinet Public Relations Office, Japan

Japan's Prime Minister Shinzo Abe met President-elect Trump Nov. 17 in New York.

Six Land Corridors

This obviously will have a big impact on the ability for the Latin American countries to put a lot of emphasis on their infrastructure development. This is not an option, this is an absolute necessity, because the world, at least concerning the trans-Atlantic part of the world economy, is facing a larger explosion than 2008. Many people have illusions about that, but we are sitting on a powder keg, in which you are stuck with the too-big-to-fail banks, those you cannot let go under because their crash would bring down the whole financial system, and whose managers you cannot put in jail for the same reason. They are much bigger today than they were in 2008; the debt and derivatives exposure is 40, 60, 80% larger. Take Deutsche Bank alone: They have a derivatives exposure of 42 trillion euros, which is four times the entire GDP of the European Union and 12 times the GDP of the German economy.

All the major too-big-to-fail banks in Europe and the United States have Deutsche Bank, with its derivatives exposure, as their derivatives counterparty. Therefore, if Deutsche Bank goes bankrupt, it would bring

down practically all of these banks. But the same condition is true for the Italian banks, and for many of the British banks after the Brexit.

In addition, you have the problem that these banks all have had dramatic losses in the last years because of criminal fines, because they have been involved in a large variety of crimes: LIBOR manipulation, sums in the three-digit billions; money laundering: HSBC. You had the Wells Fargo Bank in open fraud against its customers; the same for Deutsche Bank. And there are many other examples.

The only way you can stop these developments, so as to prevent a repetition of the 2008 explosion on a larger scale, is by implementing, immediately, the Glass-Steagall banking separation law which Franklin D. Roosevelt implemented in 1933. That has to be the absolutely necessary first step, but it has to be followed with the Four Laws of Lyndon LaRouche which I will talk about a little bit later.

Now, this situation is very dangerous and must be remedied. With the election of Trump, nothing is clarified yet. The only thing which has been eliminated is the immediate danger of World War III, but if the economic reforms which I'm now going to talk about are not implemented on a global scale, we may be back in a war danger in the very short term. So do not be at ease, but be optimistic, because the alternative economic system is already in place. And since most of the media have not paid adequate attention to that system, let me elaborate on it now, and you will see that we are actually in the middle of a huge development perspective already.

China, in particular President Xi Jinping, three years ago proposed the creation of a New Silk Road. He consciously referred to the ancient Silk Road which—2,000 years ago during the Han Dynasty—connected China with Europe, and at that time it was not only the exchange of goods such as porcelain, silk, book printing, and many other things; but it was also the exchange of culture, of ideas, and most important, of technologies—not just silk but the technology of how to make silk, how to print books, how to manufacture porcelain. At that time it led to an absolute increase in productivity, of culture. It meant a tremendous upgrading of civilization at that time.

Now, today, it would mean, and it is already meaning the exact same thing in terms of modern technologies, such as high-speed rail systems, space cooperation, fusion and fission research, and other advanced technologies. Since President Xi Jinping announced the New Silk Road in Kazakhstan in September 2013, there has been an absolute explosion of economic activity, and already, now, this whole project is 12 times larger than the Marshall Plan, which reconstructed the German economy in the postwar period. It already involves 4.4 billion people, the majority of mankind; it involves more than 100 nations and large organizations. And to just give you an idea of the enormity of what has happened in these three years, I want to give you a short overview of the different projects which are already near completion or under way.

There are presently six large land routes being constructed: This is the "belt" in the One Belt, One Road

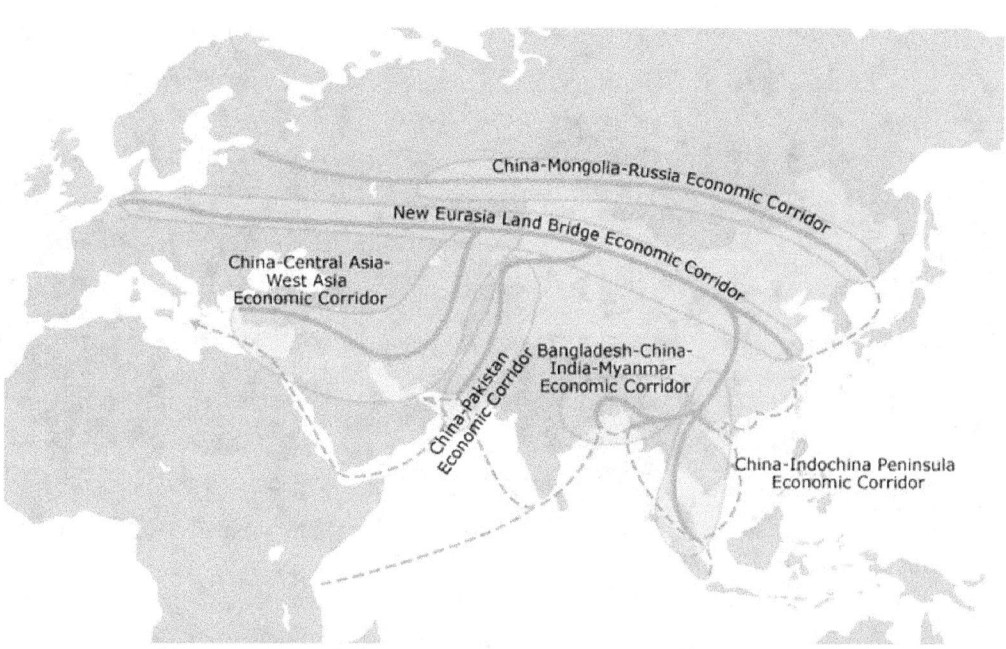

Six of the large land routes under construction as development corridors. President Xi Jinping proposed the elaborate New Silk Road project in Kazakstan in September 2013. The project is already 12 times larger than the Marshall Plan.

conception of the Chinese. Most of them are in different degrees of completion. You have the Eurasian Land-Bridge connecting China, Kazakhstan, and Russia, to Europe. Then you have the different corridors: one going from China to Mongolia to Russia; a second one from China to Central Asia to West Asia; a third one is the corridor between China and Pakistan, which China has invested $46 billion in alone. The fourth, Bangladesh, China, India, and Myanmar; the fifth, from China to Indo-China; and then you have in addition to that, the so-called 21st Century Maritime Silk Road, which is the "road" in the One Belt, One Road.

52 Special Economic Zones

From Chinese ports, this Maritime Silk Road goes through the South China Sea to the Indian Ocean, to Europe; a second route from China through the South China Sea to the South Pacific. All of these projects are based on a "win-win cooperation" with the idea that not only China profits from them, but all participating countries will, equally.

Xi Jinping made this really his personal project. Look at how many personal trips he conducted in these three years, he went to 37 countries on state visits: 18 in Asia, 9 in Europe, 3 in Africa, 4 in Latin America, and 3 in Oceania. He made free trade agreements with 11 states along the One Belt, One Road. He made bilat-

The first train of the first regular railway freight service linking Guandong Province and Germany as it is about to depart on April 15, 2016.

Xinhua/Cai Zengle

A bullet train running over a bridge on the Lanzhou-Xinjiang high-speed rail line in northwest China's Xinjiang Uygur Autonomous Region.

eral agreements with 56 states. He made joint Memorandums of Understanding for planning operations with scores of regional organizations, such as the European Union, the Central and East European Countries (CEEC), the Mekong neighboring states, the African Union, the Shanghai Cooperation Organization, the Eurasian Economic Union (EAEU), as well as ASEAN, and ASEM (the Asia Europe Meeting). This is becoming a very extensive integrated network of projects.

Part of these projects are transport lines which represent the traffic arteries through these countries. It includes the agreements for telecommunications, power plants, power grids, the creation of conditions governing locations which make landlocked areas suitable for investment as well as ocean or river sites. It is important for agriculture and development to develop these conditions. It includes the building of many new cities.

As of mid-2016, 39 cargo routes have been developed from China to Europe, on which trains arrive every week. It involves the activities of many Chinese state corporations, such as the China Railway Group Ltd., and the China Communications Construction Co. Ltd. It involves 38 large infrastructure projects in 26 countries. It involves new transport grids through land-locked areas which were completely unreachable before. It involves the upgrading of ports, and the modernization of existing infrastructure.

In the Chinese part of the Silk Road, by the middle of this year China had already built 98 new airports. Very soon it will be the case that no city in the One Belt, One Road region will be farther away from an airport than 100 km. Within China, China has already built 20,000 km of high-speed rail for running a very excellent model of high-speed train developed by China. By the year 2020, they want to have a 50,000 km high-speed rail system in China, connecting every major city through such a system. And this is intended to be extended to the other countries.

The following Chinese state companies are involved: Telecom China Unicom, China Mobile, and TDLTE Net 4G mobile telecommunication. They have now contracted for plans in 30 countries, including China, the United States, Japan, India, Saudi Arabia, and Russia.

Already in the last three years, this has led to an explosion of trade: Between 2013 and 2016 the trade volume increased by $3.1 trillion. There are $51 billion direct investments in these countries. China has created five Special Economic Zones (SEZ) across its borders: One in Dongxing on the border with Vietnam; another one Ruili on the border with Myanmar; another in Erenhot on the border with Mongolia; and another one called Manzhouli on the Russian border. Plus one in the port of Mongla in Bangladesh on the Bay of Bengal.

In addition, they have created 15 zones of economic cooperation across borders: In the northeast of China in Liaoning in the border area with North Korea; a second

A gas pipeline in Mozambique, funded by China.

Staff members in the workshop of a Chinese-funded plant in Van Trung Industrial Park in Vietnam, July 9, 2015.

one in Jilin, in the border area of North Korea and Russia; another one in Heilongjiang, with Russia; another one in the south of China in Guanxi; and a fourth one in Yunnan at the border with Vietnam; and four such zones have been built in Xinjiang on the border with Kazakhstan.

By mid-2016, China had agreements for a total of 52 Special Economic Zones (SEZ) in 18 countries along the One Belt, One Road. Three of them are already fully operational: the industrial park between China and Belarus; the second one between Thailand and China, the Rayong industrial zone; and the third is the Indonesia-China Integrated Industrial Parks. The others are in different stages of realization, such as the industrial parks in Cambodia, Vietnam, Pakistan, Zambia, Egypt, Nigeria, Ethiopia, Hungary, and four such zones in Russia.

The Far Side of the Moon

Part of this is an upgrading of the energy infrastructure. China is presently participating in 40 energy projects abroad, comprising power plants, electricity grids, and oil and gas pipelines in 19 countries, including the Central Asia-China gas pipeline which was started in 2014, and the very huge Russia-China gas pipeline which also was started in 2014. And this also includes joint nuclear projects with China and Romania, with China and Great Britain, China-Pakistan, and China-Argentina.

China is also involved in the construction of water projects in Angola, Brazil, Nepal, Pakistan, and Argentina.

To finance all of this China also initiated, together with the other BRICS countries, a completely alternative financial system, responding to the fact that in the last decades the activities of the IMF and the World Bank have betrayed criminal neglect of funding infrastructure in the developing countries, leading to the absolute underdevelopment of such continents as Latin America or Africa, or large parts of Asia. China remedied that by creating the Asian Infrastructure Investment Bank (AIIB) in 2015, which immediately, despite massive pressure from Washington not to do so, had 57 founding members, including Great Britain, Germany, France, Australia, New Zealand and Canada—very strong allies of the United States, which found it more attractive to join this bank. This bank has $100 billion of founding capital.

Then in addition, the BRICS countries created the New Development Bank in July 2015, which also had $100 billion in founding capital. By December 2014, China had already created the $40 billion New Silk Road Fund. The Maritime Silk Road Fund amounts to another $40 billion. But the largest part of this financing still comes from state banks such as the China Development Bank, which is involved in more than 900 projects for transport, energy, and raw materials in 60 countries. The China Export-Import Bank is involved in more than 1,000 projects as well—roads, rails, ports, power plants, pipelines, communications, and indus-

China National Space Administration

An artist's rendering of a base in space from which mankind can venture forth to explore.

So China, which has completely understood the science-driving ability of the space program, is now conducting probably the most advanced space program of all countries in the world. They will go to the far side of the Moon at the end of '2018, which will open up tremendous windows into space, because it's more shielded from the radiation from the Sun and from the Earth, so you will find totally new insights into the laws of the universe at that time. And China, by the year 2022 will also have, as it stands now, the only functioning space station. And they have especially invited developing countries to be part of that, so that these countries' development is not held back.

trial parks in 49 countries. The China Export and Credit Insurance Corp. also supports investments totalling $2.3 trillion in medium- and long-term projects in the high-tech area, in machine-tool building and similar areas.

Then, as a very important additional element in the new financial system, there is also the Contingent Reserve Arrangement (CRA) of $100 billion, which was the reaction of the Asian countries and the BRICS countries to the speculative attacks which caused the Asia crisis of '97, in which such speculators as George Soros speculated the currencies of a country down by 80% in one week. So the CRA has been created to counter such speculative attacks for all the participating members.

Now, at the G-20 Hangzhou summit, which this year was organized by China, China put a lot of emphasis on innovation, insisting that innovation must be the driver of the world economy. By the middle of this year, China had already signed in this spirit, Memorandums of Understanding with 56 countries for scientific cooperation, joint space research, and joint investment in research of energy environment. They have created 38 science centers and technology centers, research labs, R&D industrial parks, exchange of scientific personnel and especially an exchange of several thousand young scientists of the countries along the One Belt, One Road.

Confucian Philosophy

If you look at these developments, they are absolutely breathtaking. The first maps which were published in 2013 only showed very narrowly the One Belt, One Road line from China to Europe and the Maritime Silk Road. But if you look at the subsequent three years of development and fill in the projects which I just have named, you can see that this conception has grown exponentially. We, the Schiller Institute, are not unrelated to that, because this is a project we have pursued for more than 25 years: The so-called Productive Triangle linking the industrial zones of Western Europe with those of Eastern Europe was our answer to the fall of the Wall in 1989. Since the Iron Curtain was no longer there, we proposed economic integration of Eastern and Western Europe, and when the Soviet Union disintegrated in '91, we simply extended the so-called "Productive Triangle" to connect from the European industrial and population centers to those of Asia through infrastructure development corridors, and we called that the Eurasian Land-Bridge, the New Silk Road.

And we kept making new projects, we kept devel-

10 Productivity

EIR November 25, 2016

oping this idea further for every part of the world: for Latin America, for Africa, for the Middle East. Naturally at the time that Xi Jinping again put the perspective of the New Silk Road on the table, in 2013—which they had previously done in '96, and which had been halted because of the Asia crisis—we intensified these studies and produced a 370-page study called *The New Silk Road Becomes the World Land-Bridge*. When you look at the projects of that blueprint you can actually see that what China is doing right now by advancing all the projects I just named, will very, very rapidly to fill out the proposed projects of the World Land-Bridge.

From that standpoint, it is not a question of whether the rail line should be built from Brazil to Peru, or from Brazil to Bolivia to Peru, because all of these will be built in this larger World Land-Bridge.

At the time that this discussion initially occurred in 2013, many countries in Central Asia had exactly the same debate. They said, "Oh, this New Silk Road is not good, because it only proposes the east-west alliance between China and Europe, and we want the north-south alliance from Central Asia to Russia." This is all solved, because at the latest big conference in Vladivostok in September, and then after other conferences last month in St. Petersburg and Moscow, the full integration of the Eurasian Economic Union with the New Silk Road/One Belt, One Road Initiative is already taking place.

What is really happening is that the Chinese economic model has become the most attractive economic model in the world, because China—like Germany, by the way, in the postwar period—China also had a real economic miracle, since China was able to to speed up the economic development for which the industrialized countries had required 200 years. China did this in essentially 30 years. Therefore when China offered, in 2013, the participation in that model on a "win-win" basis, what Xi Jinping really offered is the idea that every country in the world can participate in the kind of development which China has demonstrated.

China obviously has the so-called "Chinese characteristics," which means a very strong influence of Confucian philosophy. It also means naturally a one-party system which many countries don't have. But in principle other countries can approximate this model absolutely if they focus on that which China was focussing on in its economic model, namely excellence in education, consistent emphasis on new innovation, lifelong

Xi Jinping delivering his opening remarks to the Asia Pacific Economic Cooperation (APEC) Summit in Lima, Peru, Nov. 19, 2016.

education of the labor force, and leapfrogging technology—in other words the idea that developing countries must not repeat all the steps the industrial countries have taken, but they can choose certain state-of-the-art technologies and become the best in these areas, and in that way pull the other areas of the entire economy upward.

Two Systems

The Chinese model has become so attractive that it is very, very clearly the centerpiece of a completely new dynamic, and of a strategic realignment of many countries. The fact that there is such an option now, has already changed the world. The option for development for the developing countries has not existed since the assassination of John F. Kennedy, or actually since Franklin D. Roosevelt—it existed for a short period with John F. Kennedy—but for the last 50 years, there was to the contrary the clear attempt to prevent development of the developing sector. There was the completely fraudulent thesis of the Club of Rome saying that there are "limits to growth," that we have somehow reached the end of the ability of the planet to grow. This was the basis for the creation of the Green movement. The Club of Rome and the famous book *Limits to*

Growth was based on a completely fraudulent thesis, which asserted that resources are limited, leaving out, consciously, the fact that what is a resource is entirely determined by the level of technology with which you work on that raw material. You have either a stone tool in the Stone Age, or you have a piece of iron, or rare earth mineral, something an engineer can make absolutely the most advanced things out of—that entirely depends on the level of technology which determines what kind of raw material you have.

In the time of the first two decades after the Second World War, in the United Nations you still had what was called at the time, "UN Development Decades," which was the idea that each decade would lead to an improvement of the developing countries. But that was then replaced by a completely different idea. In 1967, Pope Paul VI still produced an Encyclical which he called *Populorum Progressio*, which was the idea that every country had the right for full development.

After the paradigm shift of the Club of Rome/zero growth oligarchy, they replaced the right to development with such notions as overpopulation, sustainable development, appropriate development, which was really a synonym for no development at all.

With the New Silk Road/One Belt, One Road Initiative, however, and the alternative financial system, the AIIB and et al., you have for the first time, again the chance to completely break out of this anti-development containment. But it is also clear that the international oligarchy which was behind this zero growth movement is still waging a war against development. I'll give you one example: The so-called Saïd Business School of Oxford University published a completely absurd report in September of this year, in which they said that infrastructure investment of $10.8 trillion by China in the last decade would be the cause of a pending collapse of the economy in China, and consequently of the world economy. This conclusion is based on the idea that infrastructure is not profitable, which is absolutely ridiculous.

Pope Paul VI

When we talk about infrastructure, we're not talking about transport lines from A to B, for which the profit of such infrastructure would come out of a toll booth of a privatized highway or a privatized railroad. But we are talking about infrastructure in the context of physical economy, in which it creates the absolute necessary framework for the development of agriculture, industry, the productivity of the labor force, and the unleashing of the creative powers of mankind.

Infrastructure is only one aspect of what Lyndon LaRouche has called "physical economy," a notion which actually originated with Gottfried Leibniz, who used it for the first time in the context of the discovery of the steam engine and the increase of productivity through the input of science and technology in the production process. This tradition continued through the cameralists, through Friedrich List, the author of the Customs Union concept in Germany, and the one who very clearly in his economic theoretical writings made the distinction between the American System of economy and the English system—the fundamental difference between the national economy of Alexander Hamilton, the United States' first Secretary of the Treasury, and the free-trade advocate, Adam Smith.

The fight between these two systems has continued to the present day. It is the fight between the oligarchical system trying to get maximum profit by keeping the population down and backward, and the republican model of economy which says that the only source of wealth is the creative abilities of the population.

Out into Space

Friedrich List is, to the present day, the most known and most studied economist in China. At the Fifth World Congress in China in 2013 in Shanghai, the majority of economists said that they based the Chinese economic model primarily on the theory of List. List maintained that the development of the productive powers of labor and the resultant increased industrial capacities are much more important than so-called statistical wealth, monetary values, unlike asset-driven economies such as the United States and Great Britain. Friedrich List wrote for a contest of the French Academy of Sciences in 1837, in which he developed a vision for the future role of transport systems, which he called a space and time economy, ideas which are still completely valid for today.

Friedrich List saw in the continuous perfection of transport and communications systems, the precondition for the progress of humanity, enabling human beings to increasingly unfold the potential given to them by nature. The idea was that the more talents could exchange their ideas and collaborate in all areas, the greater progress would be in all areas of knowledge, and the more science and art would be inspired and spread to all sectors and disciplines.

And, he observed something that is completely applicable for our present jet age, noting that the easier it would be for human beings to move from place to place, the more they would save time and compress space. The more the development and efficiency of his powers would increase and utilize the material riches of nature for his purposes. He said the impact of these characteristics of space and time in economies would be demonstrated by the wealth of nations which would develop an advanced transport and communications system even if their natural environment was unfavorable. The high degree of speed, regularity and cost-efficiency of transport would facilitate new levels of the development of the mental and material productive forces.

In an almost prophetic forecast, he saw this new development orient towards the uniting of all nations in one humanity, in a republic of the planet based on the economy of mankind.

Now, it is the realization of this program of the World Land-Bridge, proceeding from the common aims of the mankind, which will be exactly the fulfillment of what List called the "republic of the planet, the economy of mankind."

Fiedrich List was a visionary. And indeed, the World Land-Bridge which he anticipated is the natural next phase in the evolution of mankind. And I want to also remind you of another great person, whose ideas are very relevant for this, and that is the great German rocket scientist Krafft Ehricke, who looked at the long

Friedrich List

arc of the evolution of the development of our planet and mankind. He outlined how life has developed out of the oceans with the aid of photosynthesis to the land; how it then came to the evolution of one species to the next, always having a higher energy-flux density in their metabolism, until you finally arrive at the human being who is distinct from all previous species, through his creative intellect, through his creative reason which is not shared by any animal or any other possible form of life.

Now, in the early development, this human being, or man, could only settle on rivers or on oceans. Then as the development continued, with the help of infrastructure, man could really open up the landlocked areas of the planet. And as the technological development became more efficient, man developed these railways, and in that sense the World Land-Bridge conception, which will open up the remaining landlocked areas of the planet, is really the logical next phase of the evolution of man.

And it does not stop here, because the next phase of the evolution is to bring this infrastructure into near space. The industrialization of the Moon which the Chinese are most advanced in pursuing, is the obvious stepping stone for larger excursions into near space, to develop a much better understanding of the laws of our

Solar system, of the Galaxy, and finally the laws of the Universe at large.

In order to solve the problems on Earth today, we all must assume the view of the astronauts, the cosmonauts, the taikonauts, who all report when they come back from space, when they look down they only see our small, fragile, blue planet, and you don't see borders, you don't see divisions, you see one mankind, and one planet.

Patriot and World Citizen

So obviously, Earth is not what the environmentalists claim, an Earthbound, closed system, but life on Earth is part of the laws which are defined in the Solar system, and in the larger scale, defined by the Galaxy. So therefore, the solutions to all the problems on our planet have to take into account what is going on in the space around us and the interaction, for example, of the Solar system with Galaxy, the impact that has on the climate and similar things.

Now we can also, from that large arc of evolution determine the necessary next step of discovery, where must we put the focus. Because mankind should not vanish—you know there are many geologists who say that mankind only appeared one second before midnight, and will disappear one second after midnight in the longer arc of the evolution of the Universe. I don't think that that is an acceptable view, because mankind is capable of mastering the laws of the Universe, and if mankind were to vanish then all the great works of our forebears, of such musicians and composers, as Bach and Beethoven, would have been in vain, because they would vanish. But mankind can go on a path of scientific and technological progress, where we will overcome all hurdles which we already can see clearly in existence, such as asteroids or developments on the Sun which affect the planet Earth. We can create a path to overcome these types of problems.

Now, let me return to what I started with. The U.S. election has created a potential to go in this direction. The absolute precondition is that the relationship between the United States and Russia and the United States and China must be put on a new basis: This is absolutely crucial for world peace, it is absolutely crucial to solve the terrible crises in Syria and Ukraine.

Therefore, in order to make all of these things a reality, we need a completely new set of international relations among nations. We have to proceed from the UN Charter which has absolute respect for the national sovereignty of all countries, which follows the principle of non-interference, and respect for the different social systems. President Xi Jinping has offered a new model of the relations among major powers which says basically, exactly that: non-interference, mutual respect for the sovereignty of the other. But these are the principles which also must guide the relations of the countries working together on the One Belt, One Road.

Therefore, we have to absolutely replace the old geopolitical view, which insists that one nation or group of nations has a legitimate interest against another group of nations, and we must replace this geopolitical idea, with a new paradigm for mankind, which must be defined by the common aims of mankind. President Xi Jinping has called that the "community of common destiny," or the "community of a common future of mankind."

This must be defined based on the idea—where do we want mankind to be in a thousand years from now? Or in 10,000 years from now? And if you think back, 10,000 years ago, from the standpoint of the development of the Universe, it's a very small part of time, so we have made a gigantic leap in the last 10,000 years. And I imagine we will make an even more gigantic leap in the next 10,000 years, and if we are going to survive as a human species, we will have to change the way we think about our kind completely. We have to think about it from the standpoint of a unified humanity.

Friedrich Schiller, who is the wonderful poet, after whom the Schiller Institute is named, was of the opinion that there must not be a contradiction between being a patriot and being a world citizen. I think that that idea is reachable in our time, because if we give every newly born child on this planet a universal education which transmits not only universal history, geology, music, science, the arts, but also a knowledge and love for the other cultures in their highest expression, of the German Classics, of Confucianism, of the Gupta period, of Cervantes, of Goya, of every high point of each culture, then these children will be able to develop the entire potential which each of them could unfold, and which in the past only very few exceptions could unfold.

The Future of Man

The immediate steps ahead to solve this crisis must be the following: We must have an immediate, global implementation of the Glass-Steagall law implemented by Franklin D. Roosevelt in 1933. We have to end the casino economy where money is the reference point as opposed to the development of the real economy and the creative potential of the population. This, then, naturally must be followed by the other three fundamental laws developed by Lyndon LaRouche which must be the creation of a National Bank in every country in the tradition of Alexander Hamilton, who created the United States with that institution; and then a credit system in every country which gives credit lines for the development of infrastructure, research & development, education, and other things which contribute to the increase of productivity and creativity of the population; and finally, we need a combination of such credit systems through a New Bretton Woods system which will be the relation among the national economies, organizing the international investments in the projects of the World Land-Bridge, which will have international clearinghouses, to compensate for the fact that nations are different. They're not all the same: you have small nations, large nations, thinly or greatly populated countries; we have countries which have a lot of raw materials, others have few or none; you have countries which have skilled labor, others have not so skilled labor forces. And you need a development perspective of at least 20, 30, 40, or 50 years,

in order to overcome that, and these clearinghouses must be what calculates that and makes sure that the bad practices of the World Bank, which demanded payback of credit before the projects were realized— that this practice is replaced by a complete focus on the completion of these projects and the fulfillment of their potentials.

So therefore, as you could see by my remarks, we are not only talking about rail lines from Brazil to Peru, or infrastructure as such. We're really talking about a completely new paradigm in the thinking of mankind. We are talking about a new era of civilization in which all human beings, every single child born on the Earth, will have the potential to develop every aspect of the potential embedded in him or her.

The future of mankind, if we are to exist, will therefore be that we will have a lot more geniuses, that it will not be that we will have a genius once in a century, like Plato, Confucius, Beethoven, or Einstein. But that a person of such a quality will be increasingly the new normal identity of civilization.

So in that spirit, I think we are hopefully at the beginning of a completely new era of mankind.

Thank you.

HELGA ZEPP-LAROUCHE IN DIALOG WITH
THE PERU ASSOCIATION OF ECONOMISTS

On the New Silk Road And World Reconstruction

The question-and-answer session immediately followed Mrs. Zepp-LaRouche's pre-recorded video presentation above. Her answers have been back-translated into English from the simultaneous interpretation into Spanish.

Question: What sort of credit system would be created for the financial platform for construction of regional infrastructure, such as the bi-oceanic rail corridor?

Zepp-LaRouche: Well, I think that this is a matter of negotiations among the participating countries, that is, Brazil, Peru, probably Bolivia, China. I think that China has already invested a lot in similar projects around the world. For example, China has invested $46 billion in Pakistan to develop a corridor connecting China to the Gulf coast. This is a project which has great potential for the future, because finally it is going to link up with India, and this is going to be one of the factors of stability in the relationship between two countries that, often in the past, have had tensions.

So, I think that China will probably participate in investing in this bi-oceanic corridor, and there obviously has to be a multilateral credit arrangement that takes into account the duration and the amount of time that it will take to build the railroad, and when it will begin to operate, and how it will be linked to other projects.

So that generally is not a big problem, so long as these credits are channeled solely to the development of infrastructure. And in that case, the investment should be measured not simply as the cost of the rail link, but

you also have to calculate the medium and long-term increase in all of the other areas of industry, agriculture, and trade, which will come about as a result of the investment in infrastructure.

Throughout history, investment in infrastructure has been the precondition and the starting point for the industrial transformation of any country. So people who say that infrastructure is too expensive, and that therefore it should be privatized—that's a mistake. Because the idea isn't to have privatized infrastructure, but rather to view infrastructure as the necessary precondition for the increase and industrial progress of the continent, and of the whole region.

Question: How can changes in economic mentality in China transform the world? How can they help address problems that have arisen under the existing economic model?

Zepp-LaRouche: I think that China, clearly, still

Xinhua/Jorge Villegas

China's One Belt, One Road Initiative has been key in diversifying bilateral trade. Shown, container shipping in the port of Valparaiso, Chile.

has a system based on a single party, and naturally it is the Communist Party—however, with Chinese characteristics. And I can tell you that it is my deepest personal conviction that, far more important than the communist aspect as such, which goes back to Karl Marx—who, by the way, was born in the same city that I come from in Germany, Trier—in any case, the Chinese Communist Party is greatly influenced by the philosophy of Confucius. Confucianism has been the state philosophy of China for thousands of years. And it has a system of values which is totally different from the system of the neoliberal monetarist theory.

Confucianism places great emphasis on knowledge, on learning throughout life, by everybody in the whole world, especially the labor force. It also places great emphasis on excellence, that one always has to try to achieve results in the best manner possible. It places great emphasis on innovation: never do the same thing twice, always progress in technological leaps, leapfrogging ahead. And China has shown that it is not necessary to repeat all of the stages of industrialization which the industrialized countries have gone through in a chronological fashion, in the way they did. Rather, you can choose and define areas in which a country can be a true world leader, and place great emphasis on the education of students in that specific area.

And that way, in a growing division of labor in a world which is increasingly specialized and differentiated on the level of the world economy, every country absolutely can profit from that system. And although there may be a multi-party system or there may be things from the old paradigm, or values from the old system that go along with globalization that only emphasizes obtaining the immediate maximum financial profit in the short term, I think that what is most profitable in the long term, and even in the medium term, is the Chinese model, which is based on the best aspects of what caused the industrial revolution in any country. Whether it be Germany, Russia, or the United States, there has always been a model which is based on physical economy. And I think that that, perhaps with greater difficulty, can be repeated in other countries.

But it absolutely can be achieved, if you have a national mission, and if that national mission is something coherent with the requirements of all mankind. And I think that this goes to the entire question of "The New Silk Road Becomes the World Land-Bridge,"—that is, that we are not talking only about transportation lines

from A to B, but rather of the total industrialization, a transformation of all continents and all parts of the planet, which so far have not fully developed.

In a certain sense, I think that once we proceed from that perspective of the totality, that humanity has to achieve a higher level of development in which every human being on the planet must participate—I think that, in that way, even a country which does not have the characteristics of China, can learn from the Chinese model about how to achieve that.

Our Historic Opportunity Right Now

Question: Helga, you are known as the "Silk Road Lady." On what principles have you based yourself, to develop that concept of a world model?

Zepp-LaRouche: Well, I think that it actually began, in a certain way, when I went as a young journalist to China in 1971; I had the opportunity to go there on a cargo ship of a company that had traded with China for over 100 years, and therefore wasn't affected by the Cultural Revolution. And I was very curious to visit and know China in the period of the Cultural Revolution—which was a very difficult moment, but I was very happy to have been able to be there.

And that experience had a big impact on me, because people were very unhappy. There were the Red Guards, who went into people's houses at night, and took them out of their houses and threw them in jail. The population was terrorized. But at the same time I encountered ancient Chinese culture, which impressed me very much, from that time on.

I developed a great interest in Chinese history and culture. And based on the general experiences of that trip, which also took me to Senegal, South Africa, Malaysia, Thailand, and Singapore—when I returned from that trip, I had the profound conviction that the underdevelopment of the developing countries was something so horrible. I could give you a lot of details of what I saw: how children slept in horrible conditions; and how a woman wanted to sell me some small thing, and I had to tell her that I didn't have any money to help her. But I returned with a profound conviction that the underdevelopment of the developing sector was something that had to be rectified.

And, fortunately, I came across the economic theories of Lyndon LaRouche, who was promoting exactly that. He was promoting true industrialization. The Third World has to be developed. And that was at the beginning of the 1970s, when the oligarchy was impos-

Helga LaRouche in Beijing in 1996, calls for a Eurasian Development Bank and "an emergency meeting of the principal nation-state powers for the purpose of establishing a new international monetary system."

ing the paradigm that began with the idea that there shouldn't be any development. They began to talk about over-population; about sustainable development, which from the very beginning really meant that there should not be any development at all. And the Club of Rome, about which I spoke earlier, and their idea that there are limits to growth, and now that there is an equilibrium and all growth must be stopped.

Lyndon LaRouche's movement opposed all of that and did in-depth studies and published development programs, such as for Africa. If you look at the map of Africa and of Latin America in the 1970s, they had a lot in common. They did not have infrastructure, or perhaps they just had one railroad which went from a mine, carrying raw materials to a port, for the colonialist exploitation of the resources. But the domestic development of infrastructure and its development was something that simply didn't exist. And that's why the idea of a transcontinental railroad between Brazil and Peru is something that is so, so crucial, because it is exactly the kind of infrastructure that every country should have, in every continent, as a precondition for industry and agriculture.

So we first did a plan for the development of Africa, and then at the end of the 1970s and beginning of the 1980s, with President Jose Lopez Portillo of Mexico, we proposed the idea of Operation Juarez.

We also worked with Indira Gandhi at the beginning of the 1980s, with a 40-year development plan for the development of India, which she began to implement. After they killed her, we worked with her son, Rajiv Gandhi.

My husband, Lyndon LaRouche, proposed a plan for the economic development of the Middle East, called the Oasis Plan. And when the Berlin Wall came down in 1989, it was clear that we had to connect Europe to Asia through infrastructure corridors, to create the same advantages of development and industry for the landlocked regions as the seacoasts, by connecting them to coastal areas and rivers.

Therefore the idea of "The New Silk Road" is an idea which we naturally supported when President Xi Jinping adopted it in 2013. We published all of those projects in a single report which is called *The New Silk Road Becomes the World Land-Bridge*.

So, in a certain way, we can say that over the last 40-45 years, we have participated directly in those projects, all on the basis of the most profound conviction that 500 years of colonialism and imperialism, and these policies, have led to many countries of the Southern Hemisphere having to accept conditions so horrible that people who live there simply cannot achieve their creative potential, which all human beings have. In the past, only a privileged elite could develop that potential, while many, many people don't even have the money or the possibilities of educating their children properly.

And I think we have reached the time in which that condition, which is an unjust condition of Mankind, can be overcome—not just in our lifetimes, but even in the next few years. Because if we look at the speed with which China has been able to progress with this idea of One Belt, One Road, and with the New Silk Road, it is truly impressive. In China, they have changed in an unprecedented manner.

So I have a lot of optimism that in the next years, we will have forgotten hunger; extreme poverty will have ended; that every child will have the opportunity to go to a good school; and we will truly be able to make a leap and achieve a Mankind worthy of that name.

Thank you very much.

Every Day Counts In Today's Showdown To Save Civilization

That's why you need EIR's **Daily Alert Service**, a strategic overview compiled with the input of Lyndon LaRouche, and delivered to your email 5 days a week.

The election of Donald Trump to the Presidency of the Untied States has launched a new global era whose character has yet to be determined. The Obama-Clinton drive toward confrontation with Russia has been disrupted--but what will come next?

Over the next weeks and months there will be a pitched battle to determine the course of the Trump Administration. Will it pursue policies of cooperation with Russia and China in the New Silk Road, as the President-Elect has given some signs of? Will it follow through against Wall Street with Glass-Steagall?

The opposition to these policies will be fierce. If there is to be a positive outcome to this battle, an informed citizenry must do its part--intervening, educating, inspiring. That's why you need the EIR Daily Alert more than ever.

TUESDAY, NOVEMBER 22, 2016

Volume 3, Number 65

EIR Daily Alert Service

P.O. Box 17390, Washington, DC 20041-0390

- Only Global Solutions, Based on New Principles, Can Work
- Tulsi Gabbard Meets with Donald Trump Regarding Syria
- Robert Kagan Throws in the Towel, Complains U.S. Is Becoming 'Solipsistic'
- War Party Moving To Preempt Trump-Putin Reset
- Syrian Army Makes More Progress in Aleppo
- Duterte Gives OK to Nuclear Power for Philippines
- Europe Will Suffer from Maintaining Russia Sanctions
- Former Chilean Diplomat Confirmed, 'We Will Joyfully Welcome Xi Jinping'
- Duterte and Putin Establish Philippines-Russia Cooperation
- François Fillon, Pro-Russian Thatcherite, Wins First Round of French Right-Wing Presidential Primary

EDITORIAL

Only Global Solutions, Based on New Principles, Can Work

Mankind's Triumph, Obama's Demise

by Dennis Speed

"Behold the Cranes of Ibykus!"
—Friedrich Schiller, from the poem,
"The Cranes of Ibykus"

Nov. 18, 2016—Although in less than 60 days the world will finally be liberated from the Presidency of Barack Obama, the best way for that Presidency to conclude would be with Obama's impeachment. The covering up for the Saudi role in 9/11, the illegal war on Libya, the resulting 2012 Benghazi affair, the arming and supplying of terrorist factions such as al-Nusra through the "Syrian anti-Assad moderate" cover; all supply a competent basis for such an action. The reason for the impeachment, however, is that for every day that Obama is left even with a fraction of the power he once enjoyed, he is capable of both provoking and launching a thermonuclear war.

True, President-elect Trump has held phone discussions with both President Putin of Russia, and President Xi Jinping of China, which may have significantly addressed, if not lessened tensions, particularly with Russia. The fact that Trump has made clear throughout the campaign that he agrees with the "Allied coalition against international terrorism" orientation put forward by Vladimir Putin at the 70th anniversary of the founding of the United Nations in September, 2015, is notable. "A great weight—"a dead hand upon the brain of the living"—has been finally lifted from the minds of the American people.

Obama's chosen successor, Hillary Clinton, has been defeated. The nightmare that began with the September 11, 2001 "Reichstag Fire" coup against the Constitution of the United States, and that was sustained through almost sixteen years, includ-

ing those of the George W. Bush, and the derivative Obama Administration, has been temporarily punctured. This is not due to the qualities of the candidate, Donald Trump, now the President-elect—although Trump's successful candidacy was a significant factor. This was due to a force that Obama, his supporters, and his proxy candidate, Hillary Clinton, unleashed themselves, and still refuse to recognize. Obama, in denial, cannot believe that his own crimes the defense of Wall Street, the assassination of Qaddafi, the Tuesday weekly killing sessions, the ignoring of the conditions of America's inner cities—have returned to defeat him. He, not Hillary, was the cause of the defeat of the Democratic Party. "The arc of the moral universe is long, but it bends toward justice." That force behind Obama's defeat is called *Nemesis*.

Flickr/Nathan Forget

Obama Stump Speech

It Weren't Local

The forces that acted in the context of the American election, Lyndon LaRouche emphasized to his associates, cannot be competently understood within the United States as such. "[The election] was not national, it was international in its entire character. And that's because Germany was big in this thing. Germany was a big factor in this thing. Putin was a big factor in this situation.

"So that's the pattern. It's not the pattern of local groups in the United States, though they have significance. But they are not something you can parcel out under categories. You have to see the larger total value. And that'll become evident, once we start to treat the economy seriously. In other words, instead of trying to figure out how to get this particular product out in a certain way and so forth, the point is, you're going to start on a global basis. What we're dealing with is a global basis.

"Now, this has been the actual condition for some time. But it has not been evident because the people have not categorized these things in the proper way. What they've done is they've accurately looked for things that they think *are* important, and they are important; but the issue here that governs, is international, *global*…

"What you're looking at is a breakdown of the entire previously existing area of life in the world. And when you see that, then you get the whole picture. I mean, the important thing on Germany—Germany was a big thing. Bill Clinton by himself was a crucial figure in this whole process. He set it up, in part.

"And so, you've got to look at this thing from the standpoint, not of what guy is important in this area or not; you've got to look at the overall picture, otherwise, you don't get the right answer."

If this assessment is understood, then the principle here called "Nemesis" is comprehended as a non-mystical, efficient acting principle in the current history—not the "current event," called the Presidential election—which has not "just occurred," but is unfolding in unknown ways as you read this.

Warning Signs

Nemesis first appeared in the form of the September 28, 2016 override of Obama's veto of the JASTA (Justice Against Sponsors of Terrorism Act) bill. Weeks earlier, Obama had been "surprisingly" forced to release the suppressed 28 pages of the Joint Congressional Inquiry's 2002 report on 9/11, which featured the long-denied role of Saudi Arabia in that attack. The Senate vote against the supposedly invincible Obama's veto of the JASTA legislation was a devastating, embarrassing 97-1, with two abstentions—Bernie Sanders and Thomas Kaine. The measure also passed by a hefty margin in the House of Representatives, and thus became law, despite Obama's instructions to prevent that from occurring. Obama was rebuffed, ignored.

Being Obama, however, he and his court chose, in their hubris, not to read the signs.

Then, as the election campaign neared its end, and candidate Hillary Clinton became ever more bellicose toward Russia—calling for a no-fly zone over Syria, which could have provoked a direct military confrontation with the Russians, for example—Americans were deeply, though perhaps silently, affected by the sheer lunacy of her approach. Even more evident to them was the arrogant disregard, by both Obama and Clinton, of the deteriorating American work-force, and of the "General Welfare" clause of the Constitution. The productive powers of the United States have been destroyed. The term "Rust Belt," carries no connotation for Obama and his court, even after the election, of a national failure of the American people by Obama, but merely the regrettable but necessary result of globalization.

Undaunted, Obama and his court of entertainers, pundits, bloggers and late-night commentators strutted on, with Hillary Clinton in tow, to what was to be an abrupt, humiliating end. "We're on the right side of history, and so are the polls," they actually said, and even continue to say.

The destruction of the American manned space program by Obama, with his moronic idea that "we've been to the Moon, so why go back?" showed him to be a threat not only to the future of the United States, but to the general welfare of mankind as a whole. That space program, resurrected, now provides the main engine for world peace and advanced economic collaboration particularly among Russia, the United States, China, and India. It is precisely with the application of space technologies to non-Earthbound processes of industrial production (such as the mining of helium-3 on the Moon, already planned by the Chinese) as well as the higher cultural platform provided by joint missions of discovery, that mankind would step above the lethal level of today's geopolitics. That was why *The Hamiltonian* headline, in response to last week's defeat of "the Obama legacy" in the November 8th election properly read: *Victory For The Universe.*

Nemesis is the principle of universal law which supplies the corrective for those guilty of the sin of Hubris. Today, Nemesis takes the form of Four Laws: drive the economy through a science driver, exemplified by space exploration, to a new platform of productivity; finance this through a national system of public credit, earmarked only for physical "great projects" designated to be improvements in the General Welfare of the nation as a whole; create a National Bank for that purpose, independent of the Federal Reserve; put those banking criminals in jail who have speculated with the nation's money, by reinstating Franklin Delano Roosevelt's Glass-Steagall, thus evaporating all the speculative debt without collapsing the banking system as such, including people's savings and entitlements.

One commentator, Daniel Franklin, author of *Pitiful Giants: Presidents In Their Final Terms*, said: "It doesn't seem fair that given Obama's popularity, he is about to be almost totally repudiated. If he can get past that...he will provide the mechanism for transition even in facilitating his own [policy] demise."

Actually, Obama's repudiation is not only eminently fair, but right, just, deserved and necessary. If there were any competitor for the worst American Administration in history to that of Obama, it would be that of his predecessors, Dick Cheney and George W. Bush. Even the pre-Civil War regime of James Buchanan would run a distant second.

Nemesis went unnoticed by the entire coterie of sophists that make up Obama's "news as entertainment" millionaires' circle. Unable to see the actual American electorate through their dense cloud of legalized-marijuana smoke, this group of deplorables deserves a further demonstration of the potential for a new paradigm-shift in the American political culture. The immediate reinstatement of Glass-Steagall, as a bipartisan "unity measure" to protect the American people, and the world, from a new financial meltdown that could, by itself, provoke a thermonuclear confrontation, would place the United States "on the right side of history"—and the hopeless, changeless Obama Administration, in its dustbin.

This article originally appeared in The Hamiltonian *of November 18, 2016.*

Our Mission and Our Task: 'Productivity. Productivity.'

Matthew Ogden: Good evening. It's November 18, 2016. My name is Matthew Ogden and you're joining us for our weekly webcast from larouchepac.com. I'm joined in the studio by Benjamin Deniston, and via video by members of our Policy Committee: Diane Sare, joining us from New York City; and Kesha Rogers, joining us from Houston, Texas.

We had the opportunity just now to have a discussion with both Lyndon and Helga LaRouche, and I think Mr. LaRouche's point is very clear. It is decisively determined that the entire reigning former system, the old system, has abruptly and decisively come to an end. But the question still remains: What will replace it? And that is far from concrete or finalized at this point. The leadership that the LaRouche PAC has delivered and continues to deliver, is the deciding factor in that—both nationally and on the international stage. It's very clear that the dynamic is now shifted towards what Xi Jinping has led in China with the New Silk Road and in collaboration with Russian President Vladimir Putin in creating a new strategic and economic international order; and that is what is determining world events right now, far beyond anything that's happening domestically from within the borders of the United States. The question is, how do we respond to that?

This was a very important week. Congress came back into session—albeit for just a couple of days; but there to greet the members of the United States Congress as soon as they returned to Washington were some of the leading activists of the LaRouche Political Action Committee. We had a day of action on the ground on Capitol Hill on Wednesday; and we definitely met a completely shaken up and much more open situation than we have faced in perhaps the last 16 years in Washington, DC.

> **People have experienced that life is just getting worse for them; and they do not have any hope in the Washington-New York establishment. You had the same phenomenon leading to the Brexit vote in Great Britain ... it was the same fundamental sense of injustice. That there is simply no more government which takes care of the common good.**

So, what we're going to do right now is play a short excerpt from a discussion that was led by Helga Zepp-LaRouche. These are remarks that she delivered to those activists as sort of marching orders before they went to Washington, DC. I think she gives a very clear overview of exactly the situation we find ourselves in, and the responsibilities that we have. So, let me play that clip for you right now:

Helga Zepp-LaRouche: [audio recording] Okay. So, first of all, I want to say hello to you. Obviously, this is a very important intervention because the election results in the United States, which many people did not anticipate, are really part of a global process. It's not something which is accounted for in all the explanations given by the US media; for the most part, they give a cover-up, or some phony explanation, like that it was the FBI who cost Hillary the election, and so forth and so on. What really is going on strategically, is that the masses of the population of the trans-Atlantic sector in particular— also in some other parts of the world, but in Europe and the United States in particular—have really had it with an establishment which has consistently acted against their interests. People in those states which are represented by the anti-establishment, they know that; because for them, the working and living conditions in the last decades one can say, but in particular in the last 15 years, have become worse and worse. People have to work more jobs; they still can't make ends meet. They have many cases where their sons and sometimes even daughters have gone to Iraq for five times in a row, to come home to be completely broken. So, people have experienced that life is just getting worse for them; and they do not have any hope in the Washington-New York establishment. You had the same phenomenon leading to the Brexit vote in Great Britain in June; which also was not just the refugees and most of the obvious issues—even though they did play a certain catalyzing role; but it was the same fundamental sense of injustice. That there is simply no more government which takes care of the common good. Whatever explanations they now come up with, this will not go away until the situation is remedied, and good government is re-established in the United States, in Europe, and in other parts of the world.

One immediate next point where the same kind of resentment probably will show is with the referendum in Italy, where on the 4th of December—that is, in two and a half weeks from now—they will have a referendum about a change in the constitution, which, as the sentiment now goes, will be also a vote against the Renzi government. Even though he promised he would resign; now, he doesn't want to resign. But in any case, this type of a process will continue until a remedy has been put in.

Now, obviously, the situation is that the Trump victory is an open question. It's not yet clear what this Presidency will become; but as Lyndon LaRouche has emphasized emphatically almost every day since the vote, this is not a local US affair. This is a global issue; it's a global international question, because one major reason why Trump won the election is because, especially in the last period, he had emphasized that Hillary Clinton would mean World War III because of her policy concerning Syria. She demanded a no-fly zone and was proposing a head-on confrontation with Russia. That was absolutely to the point, because we were on an absolutely very dangerous road to a confrontation with Russia and with China.

Trump in the election campaign had said repeatedly that he would have a different attitude towards Russia. But since he has been elected, he has been on the phone with Putin and Xi Jinping; and in both cases, said that he would work to improve the relations between the United States and Russia or respectively with China. Now that is obviously extremely important; and the other extremely important question is will he carry through with his promise on Glass-Steagall? Especially

In his speech in Charlotte, Trump had reiterated that he would immediately implement Glass-Steagall. … Bernie Sanders, Elizabeth Warren, even Pelosi said that they would cooperate with Trump if he goes for this infrastructure job-creation Glass-Steagall economic program.

in his speech in Charlotte, he had reiterated that he would immediately implement Glass-Steagall. Obviously this is the key, because only if one stops and terminates the casino economy which is really the cause for the war, can the situation be brought into shape. Obviously, all the progressives—Bernie Sanders, Elizabeth Warren; even Pelosi said that they would cooperate with Trump if he goes for this infrastructure job-creation Glass-Steagall economic program.

So, we should give the benefit of the doubt that he really means it; but we should also be aware that naturally, the entire Wall Street crowd, the neo-cons in the Republican Party will do everything possible to not have that. So therefore, we have to have this intervention to really educate the Congress and the Senate on what is really at stake. The world is now really looking, holding their breath; will there be a change in American policy for the better? Which hopefully it will; but it requires these measures: Glass-Steagall as an absolute precondition without which nothing else will work. But that is not enough, because you are not just talking about banking reform; you are talking about a completely new paradigm in the economic system. That has been defined by the Four Laws of Lyn, which everybody should really make sure that they completely understand when you are doing this kind of lobbying work. Lyn has been stressing in the last couple of days, that the key thing is to increase the productivity of the labor force; and because of neo-liberal policies, or monetarist policies of the last—one can really say decades, this productivity has gone down in the trans-Atlantic sector below the break-even point. This is why we need a national bank in the tradition of Alexander Hamilton; we need a credit policy; we need an international credit system, a new Bretton Woods system. And you obviously need a "win-win" cooperation of all nations building the New Silk Road. Also in the United States, building the Silk Road to become a World Land-Bridge.

Now, extremely important is the fourth of the Four Laws, which basically says that we cannot get an increase in the productivity of the economy unless you go for a crash program of fusion power, and you go for a crash program of international cooperation for space research. Only if you do these kinds of avant-garde leaps in productivity—like fusion technology, which brings you into a completely new economic platform with the fusion torch. You will have energy security for the whole planet; you will have raw materials security because you can use any waste and differentiate out the different isotopes and reconstitute new raw materials by putting the isotopes together in the way required. So, it's a gigantic technological leap; and the same thing goes for space technology. It will have exactly the same impact as during the Apollo program, when every investment in space technology, in rockets and other new materials, brought 14 cents back from each cent of investment. Everything from computer chips, to Teflon cookingware, to all kinds of benefits occurred as a byproduct from space research. To get the world economy out of this present condition—especially in the trans-Atlantic sector—you need that kind of reorientation towards scientific and technological progress, with increases in energy flux density. All of this Green ideology, which is really no-development ideology, has to be replaced; and the world has to go back in a direction where the real physical laws of the physical universe are the criteria for truth, and not some ideology.

Productivity and the Four Laws

Ogden: Now, Helga LaRouche also delivered an equally inspiring, but much more extensive speech at a very important conference this week that occurred in Peru. This was the 23rd National Congress of the Association of Economists of Peru, that was held

NASA

The Saturn V rocket launching the Apollo 11 mission on July 16, 1969 with three astronauts, two of whom were the first to reach the surface of the moon.

A gigantic technological leap ... will have exactly the same impact as during the Apollo program, when every investment in space technology, in rockets and other new materials, brought 14 cents back from each cent of investment. ... To get the world economy out of this present condition— especially in the trans-Atlantic sector—you need that kind of reorientation towards scientific and technological progress, with increases in energy flux density.

---

in conjunction with the APEC meeting which is occurring over this weekend in Lima, Peru. The title of the conference was "The Peru-Brazil Bi-Oceanic Train; the Impact on the Economy of the Amazon Region and the Country." So, this is Peru-Brazil transcontinental railroad. Helga LaRouche's presentation was the keynote address; and she delivered it at the opening session. It was titled, "The New Silk Road Concept; Facing the Collapse of the World Financial System." This APEC summit which will be occurring this weekend, will be hosting world leaders including Vladimir Putin and Xi Jinping. There has been a major surge in interest and engagement between China and these countries of South America, around the idea of expanding the New Silk Road into South America. That would also obviously have to include North America. This is the vision that Helga LaRouche has been emphasizing, and what she laid out in a very inspiring way in this speech in Peru; the idea of "The New Silk Road Becomes the World Land-Bridge." The organizers of that conference—this national congress of economists, the economists' association in Peru— drafted their own copy of a 60-page pamphlet that they distributed to all the participants of this conference, that was based on excerpts from this report by *EIR*—"The New Silk Road Becomes the World Land-Bridge." It also included a printing of Lyndon LaRouche's Four New Laws concept. So, this is obviously a very significant event; and the fact that it's happening in conjunction with the APEC summit at this moment in history, is very important. We hope to make the proceedings of that conference available to viewers of this website.

And, there are some much deeper scientific points that have got to be addressed. 1. The understanding of what Alexander Hamilton actually did; and 2. what Lyndon LaRouche's science of economics defines as real productivity from the standpoint of increases in energy flux density. So, I think that sets up the discussion that we can have here right now. Ben, Diane, Kesha, and I think we should maybe expand from there.

Benjamin Deniston: I think it's very important that Mr. LaRouche, increasingly in the last couple of months, has said over and over again, "Productivity; productivity; productivity." We have to start thinking about not just providing jobs, not just providing needed infrastructure projects. I think it's worth making a distinction between on the one side things that are just needed to maintain what we have. We have a massive deficit just to maintain the standard—I think the appropriate term is "platform" as Mr. LaRouche had introduced a couple of years back —about how to think about infrastructure and the real development of a national territory in a scientific way. You have a certain platform of activity, a standard of activity level that maintains a specific level of existence for your society, directly connected to the potential relative population density of your society. We should always be looking to push to higher and higher platforms, higher levels of activity. Our current platform is degraded; much of the infrastructure we live upon was built largely under Franklin Roosevelt and a few spurts of activity following him on that. So on the one hand, yes, we need to rebuild some of these things. Our existing dam systems, transport systems, even soft infrastructure like health care systems are in need of repair. But we also need to push to a higher level; we need to go to a new platform which has higher degrees of productivity per capita. Higher degrees of ability to support a larger population in new area, new territories of the country; increase the productivity of existing territories, and that begins to create real growth. You're not going to get real growth just by rebuilding what you have; although you need to

> **You have a certain platform of activity, a standard of activity level that maintains a specific level of existence for your society, directly connected to the potential relative population density of your society. We should always be looking to push to higher and higher platforms, higher levels of activity.**

do that, because we've been letting this decay for decades now.

But you also need to create real economic value, real economic growth. And that goes to this issue of, are you increasing the productive powers of your labor force? Are you increasing the ability of your productive sector to produce the physical goods needed to support society more efficiently and at higher qualities with less physical input per capita, you could say? Can you measure those kinds of steps of growth? Are you taking that metric into account? That's critical right now; and it's worth recognizing that we've been living in a post-industrial policy for many years now. This whole idea of the services economy, that somehow we can support ourselves by creating jobs in services; where we take turns washing each other's laundry. I make you a cup of coffee; you make me a hamburger. That doesn't actually create qualitative changes in the ability of society to sustain more people at higher living standards. You're just trading service work back and forth.

So in all of this, we need to have a serious re-focussing on what are the essential principles of human economic growth? And that's why Mr. LaRouche's Four Laws in totality is so crucial. That's why I thought it was very good in Mrs. LaRouche's orientation into our deployment into DC, she made a very clear point on Mr. LaRouche's fourth law—this fusion driver program. These are the kinds of things that you might employ a relatively small part of the population in that specific endeavor; but you're pushing the frontiers of engineering capabilities, scientific capabilities. That actually has the most important radiating effect on the entirety of the economy, the entirety of the productive capabilities of the labor force.

You absolutely need this science driver, this high-technology, high capital-intensity driver program to really push the whole program forward. The depth of the crisis that we've gone into just makes it that much more important that we have that element up there, front and center. Since Mr. LaRouche put out this Four Laws document, he has also obviously been increasingly focussed on the role of space in that focus, in that goal. That is another absolutely critical element of this. It was not an incomprehensible or miraculous thing that

John F Kennedy's Apollo program had such a massive spin-off effect in terms of payback to the US economy from the investments that were made. The studies not that long after the project finished, were already showing a 14-1 payback in terms of the totality of increases of productivity of industries that were not part of the space program; but acquired technologies. Precision engineering capabilities; high-precision control systems for production; various things that were created out of necessity to make this super-advanced Moon mission work. But that increased the ability of mankind generally to be more productive in his production capabilities. That was then able to be applied throughout the economy generally.

So, those are the kinds of things that we absolutely need right now; not just repairing our existing degraded infrastructure. We're going to have to do that, sure; but how do you create the growth where you can afford to do that, and afford to make completely new investments? Part of this infrastructure discussion should be opening up new territories of the country. A major part of this pamphlet that we put out, and a huge part of Mrs. LaRouche's focus, has been new cities. You've got huge territories in the United States that are not developed. Let's develop the nation; let's expand new territories; let's create huge areas of new growth. That's the kind of stuff that's going to drive the whole process forward. We're in a real need for some precise, clear, authoritative leadership on these issues, because these things are not understood. We're not just going into this in a vacuum; we have a completely broken-down system; not just in the financial sector, but in the physical economy, too. So we need clear, precise, immediate action. We don't have years for somebody to figure this thing out over time; people's lives are on the line right now in terms of what's needed to turn the US economy around.

The Purpose of the Presidency

Diane Sare: Well, I'd like to just put this in a context; because we're not having a discussion here in the abstract. And I want to go back to what Mr. LaRouche did in the 1970s with the creation of the Fusion Energy Foundation, and his role in being brought into a team to create a Presidency. I want to be very clear with the people watching this that what we are doing is not an academic discussion of nice things that we, sitting in a little corner, want to do. Mr. LaRouche—as you heard from what Ben laid out—had a very clear conception of the necessity of fusion energy at that time. Also, people

remember the Jimmy Carter Presidency; small is beautiful. I think we were talking about global cooling back then, and now it's global warming. What we needed to do, in collaboration with Edward Teller, was to take the Mutually Assured Destruction doctrine off the table. The only deterrent to a nuclear war between the US and the Soviet Union was who could blow up the world more times over. What happened was, in the process of this, Ronald Reagan as a candidate and then as President, was recruited to this idea; and I think we've been told there a number of things which Mr. LaRouche was working on with the Reagan administration. Not the least of which was the SDI, which the Soviets rejected and Reagan announced, which led in a not-so-indirect way to the Berlin Wall coming down. Also, there was discussion of a meeting between President Reagan and Indira Gandhi, the prime minister of India who was a leader of the Non-Aligned Movement. Reagan, as people recall, was shot in '82; Indira Gandhi was assassinated; Mr. LaRouche was put in prison. I'm not saying that to say that we're worried about it; there's all kinds of questions of security and safety. But my point is that LaRouche personally has played a major, important role in shaping the institution of the Presidency; and his incarceration was timed for when we had earlier another such great opportunity, which was when the Soviet system collapsed economically, as he had warned it would. He was in prison, and his wife Helga Zepp-LaRouche put on the table with him the Productive Triangle and so on. We know what happened; that was sabotaged by a series of wars. The Balkans; the first Iraq War; we later had 9/11 and so on.

What we are doing today is to shape the American nation in participation with what is a New Paradigm; which LaRouche and his wife personally have been very much involved in creating. Two years ago, Mr. La-Rouche announced that we should move the center of our American operations to New York City; which was done. In the last three or four months, we have begun circulation of a newspaper appropriately titled *The Hamiltonian*. I'll just say I found it ironic that the *New York Times* today has these headlines about infrastructure. They also have articles about how school children in Estonia and Latvia were terrified that Hillary Clinton was going to drag them into the middle ground of a war between NATO and Russia. It's very interesting.

The big title on *The Hamiltonian* this week is "We Are Facing a New Epoch for Mankind"; the subtitle is "The New York Times Has Become Irrelevant." So, they may be scrambling to make themselves relevant. But what you also see, is we have printed now, four weeks in a row, Mr. LaRouche's Four Laws. They have no excuse to be so idiotic on their proposals; both for how you fund this, and how they're thinking about it, which is all domestic. The world now, what Mrs. La-Rouche described in her speech in Peru, was that Xi Jinping made his announcement of this in September of 2013. In those three years, he travelled to 37 nations; he made bilateral agreements with 56 nations; 39 new cargo routes have been opened. These are major international transportation corridors; 98 airports. The magnitude of this completely boggles the mind. It really is in keeping with what Hamilton would have envisioned; what you saw with Henry Carey, or John Quincy Adams in terms of their role in the United States. And I would say geographically, if you could step away, if you could get on a space ship and look at the Earth from a distance; or just take out a globe and look at what the United States is, where we are between the Atlantic and the Pacific. What North America is, and South America now getting involved, we have a great opportunity before us to play an absolutely strategic role in this. Our intent is to bring this about, which is why it's so crucial that everybody watching this, makes it a point to master the principles in Mr. LaRouche's Four Laws. Particularly the fourth principle, and also particularly the principle of credit; which is in a sense tied to the increase of productivity. We're not going to fund infrastructure by tolls; we're not going to build a new bridge, a tunnel under the Hudson and charge people a toll and that's going to pay for it. No, if your population is able to produce orders of magnitude more than it is currently producing, that is a net increase in the wealth of the nation. It has nothing to do with tolls, or tickets for public transportation; which are all sort of a form of tax farming and looting.

I do want to underscore: 1. The role of Lyndon La-Rouche in shaping the Presidency; 2. That this is going to occur from Manhattan; the entire transition seems to be being organized from Trump Tower on Fifth Avenue in New York City. It is incumbent on all of us to raise this to the appropriate level of discussion and to not tolerate anything smaller.

> **We're not going to fund infrastructure by tolls; we're not going to build a new bridge, a tunnel under the Hudson and charge people a toll and that's going to pay for it. No, if your population is able to produce orders of magnitude more than it is currently producing, that is a net increase in the wealth of the nation.**

Space Science and Classical Music

Kesha Rogers: Just to follow up on that, another important aspect of the fight waged by Mr. LaRouche and his wife Helga— going back to the 1970s around the fight that you just mentioned, Diane, of the Fusion Energy Foundation—was the fight against this apparatus of a zero-growth or no-growth culture. He was very instrumental with Mrs. LaRouche and also their collaboration with space pioneer Krafft Ehricke—who we've mentioned a lot— on taking on this degeneracy of the attack on population reduction that was being promoted and continues to be promoted to this day. Many people may remember that there was a book put out in the 1970s by two men, Dennis Meadows and Jay Forrester. Jay Forrester just died recently at 98 years old. He was instrumental in putting out the computer models which indicated that there was a certain relationship between the limited resources on Earth and the production of food to how many people you can sustain on Earth and so forth. This is something that Mr. LaRouche has taken directly in terms of this is an attack on the human identity, an attack on the real productivity based on the creative potential of the human mind and LaRouche's model has been brought up on the increasing of the energy flux density of your economy per capita, and per land area.

I think it's really important right now to look at the fact that Mr. LaRouche sees this fight as a complete shift in the global direction of mankind; unifying mankind on a level that nations have never been unified on before. I thought it was important that yesterday, we had a discussion with Mr. LaRouche —Ben, myself, and others from the leadership team; and one thing that he brought up was the integration of the space program and the development of space research, space science, and the exploration of space to Classical music—which we're really defining in the development of our Manhattan Project, which is really shaping our organization across the country and internationally. You have seen a culture which is completely degenerated under the Bush-Obama Presidencies. You take the inspiration, the culture which shaped the identity of the fight and the vision that led President John F. Kennedy to implement the space program in the way he did. The fact that he brought in people like Pablo Casals into the White

Max Planck Institute

Wendelstein 7-X, the world's largest experimental fusion reactor, successfully confined hydrogen plasma when it was first switched on in December 2015. It was built in Germany by the Max Planck Institute.

House; that this classical identity and classical culture was very instrumental throughout the space program, by people such as space pioneer Wernher von Braun and various others working with him. Some of these scientists who came with von Braun, like Krafft Ehricke and others, from Germany, who helped to shape the US space program. It's interesting; you compare that to what you've seen under Bush. Who did he bring into the White House during his inauguration? I think it was Ozzy Osbourne; rock music, heavy metal. Then you had Obama bringing in Beyoncé, not to mention the other very degenerate cultural figures that he has brought in. So, I think what Mr. LaRouche is saying around this is extremely important.

I think it's also important to look at the space program and the integration of the classical culture as the expression of a higher identity of what it means to be human, and the inspiration and optimism that's been missing from the population. There's a few more things we can say on this; I think it's also important to recognize the importance internationally of what China is doing. We can say more on this later, but the fact is that when you talk about inspiration and optimism, we have now the Shenzhou 11 space crew, the crew in China who just docked 33 days ago to the Tiangong 2, the space lab

for China. They're doing experiments that are quite phenomenal; but what they're really expressing—they're going to continue doing these experiments in space. One of the things we saw back in 2013, when you had the astronauts docking the first space lab for China, videoing this and beaming it back to Earth; and 60 million children watching it. They're going to do something similar for this space experiment. This is something that we have to go back to right now; the space program is not just some abstract thing on the side for gurus who like it. We have to make it part of the culture; we have to make it something that inspires and uplifts the population again, but is instrumental in the development of the increases of the productivity of society and increases in the platform. So that means that the population has to come to a higher level of understanding of their identity; and the way to do that is really an integration of culture, as Mr. LaRouche has made clear.

Productivity Again

Sare: I just wanted to add one quick thing on that note; which is a musical question actually—if you think about a symphony orchestra or a chorus and the role that individuals play as part of that body; where the whole is definitely greater than the sum of its parts. Were we to launch a transformation of society along the lines of what Mrs. LaRouche outlined in Peru; that is, the US to become integrated in part of the Belt and Road program, then I think we would quickly discover that we actually don't have enough people in this country. So that all the things that people are afraid about, about who's going to be excluded, who's going to be deported, etc.; you will find yourself looking at your fellow human beings with new eyes because of the creative potential of each individual which will be necessary to transform the nation and the world in the immediate future.

Ogden: Ben was just referencing some of Mr. LaRouche's early writings on economics which really get to the question of how do you measure productivity. This is not just raw labor power; this is not just the number of jobs. But it is the question of generation upon generation, can you produce more than is consumed? But can you do it in a way where the power of the human species actually is transformed almost as a species characteristic, step by step? I've found it very inspiring that during those opening remarks that we played by Helga, she went back to the discussion of what we used to call the isotope economy. What power can mankind wield if we penetrate not just to the molecular level, but to the very atomic level? Fission power is breaking apart the atom; fusion is an entirely different matter, where you actually have the ability to create new elements. You have the ability to create new isotopes of any given elements, which have very differing characteristics. It's the promise of Promethean fire, which mankind has been working towards over millennia; but we have not yet achieved. This is an inspiring subject, but the ability of mankind to wield power at the very basic level of the fabric of matter; that's an entirely new power.

Deniston: Yeah, and it's a huge subject that could be probably taken up in much more detail. It really goes to the question of what is a resource? What do we consider as a resource; and how that continually changes as mankind develops. Once you go to this level of an isotope conception of resources, we don't use up isotopes. When you use petroleum or wood, anything you use—unless you're actually doing fission and fusion, when the total amount of matter you're working with is very small—you're not actually destroying the elements themselves. You might be acting on a state of organization that's been created. We might be looking for certain states of organization to utilize the properties of that as a resource at a certain point. But I think this goes right to the issue of the isotope economy, the intimate connection with energy flux density where we could begin to create those states of organization ourselves; or work with lower states of quality of concentrations of ores and various things. Where things that were not economical before to do, or not even possible to do before; if you get a higher energy flux density, a higher

> China has said, "Hey, United States! If you want to quit this geopolitical, Nineteenth Century crazy game and get to some serious discussion about creating a future for mankind, that's what we're doing. So, if you want to work with us, we'd be happy to cooperate with you in a serious, honest investment and development for our nations."

energy throughput, you can begin to manage in a completely new way. Separating the quality of resource elements that we want; organizing them in new ways.

Right now, a family needs to work three or four jobs just to not get by month-to-month, and not be able to afford health care, not be able to afford education. We need a society where one job can sustain a significantly sized family and provide these kinds of benefits—higher education, health care, and have free time for arts, for recreation, for developing the cultural mental powers of your family and yourself. How you're going to get to that point is going at these issues we're talking about here, of actually increasing the productivity of the labor force as a whole; the productive powers of the labor force as a whole. Pushing these kinds of science driver, technology driver programs that make these kinds of breakthroughs.

Mr. LaRouche's point on this as a new focus that he's put on this in the recent period, is really critical. We got to raise this discussion to not just jobs, but productivity. What's your ability to produce things? If we're serious about turning the economy around. It's kind of been referenced here and there, but we have allies in doing that. It's not just going to be completely on our own shoulders. We have to decide to do it, but China has said, "Hey, United States! If you want to quit this geopolitical, Nineteenth Century crazy game and get to some serious discussion about creating a future for mankind, that's what we're doing. So, if you want to work with us, we'd be happy to cooperate with you in a serious, honest investment and development for our nations." Many other nations are rallying around China in their effort to do that; so that's there as a critical support point, if the United States makes this shift. These are the critical issues that we've got to put on the table and fight out.

And again, Mr. LaRouche's Four Laws, as he said, is a central organizing document around that whole perspective.

Rogers: Yeah, it's also important to note that as Mr. LaRouche said, in the calling for the implementation and enactment of the Four Laws that he's put on the table as an urgent necessity, Glass-Steagall being the first and urgently needed measure, is not an option or a compromise with the Wall Street bankers. He indicated that it has to be the Franklin Roosevelt Glass-Steagall; and it can't be a watered-down Dodd-Frank compromise or anything of that nature. There's only one way you're going to wipe out this casino economy, Wall Street speculation; and I think that goes the same way for the measures needed with the development of the types of density and increase in energy source and fusion economy as Mr. LaRouche is calling for. There's a lot of compromise out there about that, too. "Fusion is a long way away; it's never going to happen. The politicians aren't going to let it happen." All of this stuff.

I attended a space conference this week; and one of the things that was being promoted in terms of deep space exploration was solar-electric power. "Yes, we agree; nuclear, increase in fusion sources is most important, but it's not practical. So, we're going to go with this." Or, "We're going to push this, because it's probably something we can get through Congress." That's the most insane thing you can think of. When they talked about carrying cargo into space would be 2-3 years, is that real productivity? How are you going to advance mankind's exploration into space and the ability to actually go out to a Moon mission as a base? And a Mars mission? Also, just increasing what Ben was just discussing in terms of our ability to increase our resources here on Earth. The mining of Helium-3 on the Moon and various other resources that we've talked about.

Once again, the point was, a lot of people want to compromise on these things. There cannot be compromise because there is a global shift underway; and that global shift is requiring an increase in the highest levels of scientific development that has to be implemented immediately. This is why Mr. LaRouche's fourth law in terms of fusion driver program, is something that—just like Glass-Steagall—cannot be compromised on; and is absolutely fundamental for pushing forth the breakthroughs which are necessary.

Ogden: It is incumbent on all the activists, all the viewers of this broadcast, to master the contents of Mr. LaRouche's Four Laws document. This might seem like a short document, but it's a very dense document; and a lot of the subjects that Ben has brought up here today in terms of the definition of economic productivity and what the nature of mankind is. Kesha, what you were saying; there really are no limits to growth. This is not some kind of thing where when we reach our carry-ing capacity, that will be it. It's mankind transforming its own species; transforming the universe, and transforming our relationship to the universe. That's what's addressed in this policy document by Lyndon LaRouche. You have to set the bar that high; it cannot be any lower than that level from which you're going to effect the kind of revolution in policy that's necessary for the entire planet at this time.

So, we have a lot of work to do. Our role is—and has always been—to shape the institution of government of the United States from the very highest level. This is not coming in from the outside; this is not a voice calling in the darkness. This is working with the leadership of the nations of the planet and creating the dynamic that you now see taking over. This has been decades in the making; but I can guarantee you, Lyndon and Helga LaRouche have played a role that has been central to this reality now coming into being. I'm talking about the New Silk Road; I'm talking about this trilateral relationship between Russia, China, and India, creating a new dynamic on the Eurasian continent. Everything that's happening in South America right now, is something that Lyndon LaRouche was personally involved in over decades; and now South America coming into the New Silk Road and joining this new World Land-Bridge is something that is very real.

Nothing is determined; but our role is to continue that fight inside the United States, and to make this a reality — "The United States *Joins* the New Silk Road." We put it in the present tense for a reason.

So, I'd invite Diane, Kesha, if there's anything concluding that you'd like to say before we close out the show?

Sare: I think one great benefit of launching this recovery and increasing the productivity is all the states which just voted to legalize marijuana, will have second thoughts about that.

Deniston: We want high productivity, and it doesn't mean that.

Ogden: OK. We'll take that as a concluding point here. Please stay tuned. We will make the full speech that Helga delivered in Peru available. Also, we will be producing a feature video—about 10 or 15 minutes in length—on the content of the Four New Laws. That fleshes out some of the Hamiltonian aspect of that; and it's an educational tool to teach yourself and to teach everybody else real economics. So stay tuned for that; that will be coming to the website soon.

Optimism and Human Productivity

by Robert Ingraham

Nov. 20—The election of Donald Trump as the next President of the United States has now placed the human race at a moment of great, unprecedented potential change. Since the United States, constitutionally, is governed by a Hamiltonian Presidential System, much will depend, in the weeks and months ahead, on the actions and initiatives to be taken by the new President. Yet, our job, that is, the responsibility of what it means to be an American citizen, must be to define—and to fight for—a clear approach as to what the nature of this change must be. Ultimately, what shall be decisive in this battle will be the willingness, among a growing number of Americans, to study and think through the implications of the principles set forth by Lyndon LaRouche in his "The Four New Laws to Save the U.S.A. Now!"[1] as well as their willingness to take up the challenge posed by Mr. LaRouche to study, discuss and master the principles set forth by Alexander Hamilton in his four great *Reports* of 1791-1792.[2]

Alexander Hamilton

Let us be very clear. The American election which took place on November 8 did not represent a victory of the Republican Party over the Democratic Party. Any truly honest assessment recognizes that the unlikely Trump victory signified a near-violent repudiation of the leadership and elites of both parties. It was a vote against the four-term Bush/Obama policy of endless wars, Wall Street bailouts, confrontation with Russia, and the economic rape of the American people. In achieving the Republican nomination, Mr. Trump campaigned against the leadership of his own party, and during the general election campaign many of those Republican Party elites, including members of the Bush family, either openly or covertly rallied in support of Mrs. Clinton's candidacy, a candidacy also fanatically backed by Barack Obama. Emphatically, the vote which took place on November 8 was a vote to expunge the entirety of the policies and the leadership of the last sixteen years of both George W. Bush and Barack Obama.

During the campaign, Mr. Trump repeatedly signaled his intention to rebuild American industry and infrastructure, while he also emphatically endorsed a return to the principles of Glass-Steagall banking regulation and a revival of the U.S. space program shut down by Obama. All of these proposals are laudable. Since the election, many others have weighed in with proposals on how these and like objectives should be achieved.

How is the educated American, or anyone else for that matter, to navigate these seas, to be able to discern the difference between crackpot schemes, which will only worsen the banking and economic crisis, and sound economic practices which will engender a true economic recovery? This is where the issue of Alexander Hamilton and the principles enunciated in LaRouche's "Four Laws" come into play.

I. Hamilton, Hamilton, Hamilton

If one wishes to differentiate between those who merely pay lip service to Alexander Hamilton and those who are striving to implement a verifiable Hamiltonian policy, the only means by which to do so is to

---

1. www.larouchepub.com/lar/2014/4124four_laws.html
2. E-book: https://www.amazon.com/Vision-Hamilton-Hamiltons-Reports-LaRouches-ebook/dp/B01MEG8J96
Paperback edition: http://bit.ly/HamiltonsVision

read Hamilton himself. No "interpretations" of Hamilton by so-called "experts" or historians will suffice. This is the reason why the singular most important initiative which could be undertaken at this moment is to recruit Americans—20,000, 100,000, one million, or more, into Hamilton reading groups. To discover and to talk through the basis upon which a future-oriented economic recovery might be built.

In his 1792 *Vindication of the Funding System*, Hamilton denounces "land-jobbers," "stock-jobbers," and "jobbers of any other kind." In modern usage, simply substitute the word "speculator" for "jobber." In his two *Reports on Public Credit*, Hamilton defines the basis for a sound legitimate banking and credit system. He defines not merely the specifics of his proposal but the principles upon which it must be based. He makes short shrift of all unsound and hare-brained schemes. In one sense, his is a system of sound conservative (non-speculative) banking. Far more important, however, is his insistence as to the role to be played by that banking system. He does not deny to anyone, including the bank investors, a modest honest profit, but the paramount intention of the Credit System which he prescribes is to provide the means for a rapid industrial, agricultural and scientific advancement of the nation. That is its true purpose.

In his *Report on Manufactures*, following a discussion of the benefits that

White House/Chuck Kennedy

President Obama and Michelle Obama (right) host George W. Bush and Laura Bush in the White House, May 2012.

A decaying former factory in Newark, New Jersey.

his plan will provide to American manufacturing and agriculture, Hamilton states: "To cherish and stimulate the activity of the human mind, by multiplying the objects of enterprise, is not among the least considerable of the expedients, by which the wealth of a nation may be promoted." Thus, Hamilton places the issue of increasing *Human Productivity* at the center of his intention. To "cherish and stimulate the activity of the human mind," to "multiply the objects of enterprise"—this is the singular objective for all great economic and banking policy, and it is this that must become the guiding principle today.

II. A Global Policy

Wall Street and its failed policies were repudiated in this election. Fortunately, America does not need to "begin from scratch" in the creation of a new financial and economic system. This is already underway. On November 17, 2016, Mrs. Helga Zepp-LaRouche delivered a speech,[3] titled "The New Silk Road Concept, Facing the Collapse of the World Financial System," to the 23rd National Congress of the Association of Economists of Peru. Since the entirety of that speech is reproduced elsewhere in this issue of

---

3. See the transcript of the speech in this issue of *EIR, page 5.*

http://www.gwadarport.gov.pk

Pakistan's strategically important Gwadar port, being developed by China as part of the $46 billion Economic Corridor linking the two countries.

EIR, it is not necessary here to delineate all of the crucial elements that Mrs. Zepp-LaRouche discusses. However, since our current topic is the urgent necessary actions which must now be taken in the United States, referencing a few of the implications of that report will be most helpful.

As Mrs. LaRouche emphasizes, Americans must realize that what we are now dealing with is not an "American" crisis, nor is there merely an "American" solution. Economically, hundreds of millions around the world are facing poverty, hunger, lack of health care, underemployment, homelessness, lack of fresh water and other extreme conditions. At the same time, the financial/banking crisis is gripping the entire trans-Atlantic world, including Wall Street, London and the entirety of the European Union. Exemplary is the case of Deutsche Bank, one of the world's largest banks, which has a derivatives exposure of 42 trillion euros, four times the Gross Domestic Product of the entire European Union. JPMorgan Chase, Citigroup, and Wells Fargo are all in similar, if not quite as extreme, circumstances.

At the same time, just as the problem is global, the solution is emerging globally. If one looks at what China has initiated over just the past four years, the pathway out of this crisis begins to emerge. In 2014, at China's instigation, 57 nations joined to form the Asian Infrastructure Investment Bank (AIIB). The bank began operations one year later. During this same period, China also played a key role in the creation of both the BRICS New Development Bank (NDB) and the Silk Road Fund. These three institutions, combined, have a market capitalization of $240 billion, and, together with several of China's state-owned financial institutions, what they have accomplished over just the past 24 to 36 months has been staggering. As of today, it is estimated that the total amount of new investment in the physical economy, throughout the spheres of both the BRICS nations and the "One Belt-One Road" regions, including rail lines, electricity generation, port development, highways, communications, hydro-electric power, is already twelve times larger than the post-World War II Marshall Plan. It is massive, and it is continuing to grow.

What is already underway is an unprecedented historic breakthrough of global physical economic development. If one studies the economic projects discussed by Mrs. LaRouche in her speech, which themselves represent only a small portion of what is now being built, the picture is breathtaking. Global economic development is now taking off in a way never before seen in history. The possibilities are limitless. Greater projects than one can imagine are within reach and ready for realization. It is already happening. Will the United States remain out in the cold, missing this opportunity? All President-elect Trump has to do, to fundamentally change the course of human history, is to have the United States join in this process as a full partner.

China's Experimental Advanced Superconducting Tokamak (EAST).

tech.sina.com.cn

III. Human Productivity vs. Monetary Productivity

The absolute pre-condition for the United States to make this turn in policy is the immediate re-enactment of Glass-Steagall legislation. However, it must be mandatory that what is enacted is the *full Franklin Roosevelt Glass-Steagall Law*, not some watered down version, labeled as a "new" or "modern" Glass-Steagall or some other such sophistry.

The era of unbridled financial speculation—gambling—must end immediately.

The regulated commercial banking system must be returned to its Hamiltonian intention.

In this regard there are three terms which should be examined: "productivity," "risk," and "leverage."

For many modern Wall Street "investors," productivity is defined purely in monetary terms, and that is the way it is normally discussed in the nation's financial publications. If a factory, or any other enterprise, can be made to produce more or cheaper goods, with the same labor force, the same expenses and the same level of investment, this is labeled as an increase in *productivity*, i.e., a greater monetary return. Such results can also be accomplished through maintaining the current levels of production or sales while decreasing labor costs, R&D, capital investment, etc. The result is the same: a larger monetary return.

In his *Report on Manufactures*, Hamilton defines productivity in opposite, scientifically precise, terms. Productivity is measured by an increase in the "labor power" of the individual worker, or, more precisely, by an increase in the productive powers of the nation as a whole. Objects of production—including the people—are never destroyed or looted to increase monetary profit. Rather, investments in science, technology, as well as in such things as education, are prioritized so as to produce a greater cognitive and scientific power within society. This is not mystical. All one has to do is to look at, for example, John Kennedy's Apollo Project to begin to grasp the type of approach which is needed.

True productivity is always long term. It is defined as an investment in the future, and often many of the benefits will not be realized for one or two generations. None of the investments will return short term monetary profits. This is why get-rich quick financial shysters must never be allowed anywhere near key policy-making influence. It is the responsibility of government to deploy and utilize its awesome power to ensure the necessary upward breakthroughs.

Crash science projects, such as fusion energy or the Chinese mission to the far side of the Moon, are the epitome of this notion of investing in the future, transformative investments and accomplishments which will radically enhance mankind's power over nature and mankind's understanding of the universe. It is precisely a commitment to these "frontier" endeavors which defines a true understanding of productivity. This is why, today, any "infrastructure" program which concentrates on fixing roads or upgrading our water and electricity grid, while denying or denigrating the urgent necessity for a massive Apollo-style space program, would represent an horrendous error.

Fundamentally, the crucial issue in economic policy is an intention to develop the potential for the emergence of genius within the population, the emergence of true creativity—the development of the *Human Mind*. In this way, human culture advances and the actual nature of the human species becomes manifest.

Risk

China's current economic policies are routinely attacked by many among the London and Wall Street fanatics as "unsustainable," and many point to the volume of non-performing loans that have been extended by Chinese banks. There is a great deal of talk of dangerous financial *risk* in the Chinese banking system.

In truth, there are hundreds of billions of dollars in "non-performing" loans that Chinese banks have extended to various manufacturing and other business enterprises. At the same time, Chinese banking investments in various industrial, agricultural, energy and other physical economic projects now total 44 percent of China's Gross Domestic Product, a figure far higher than anywhere in the trans-Atlantic world. Chinese officials, however, have repeatedly stated that they view the issue of Risk far differently than their counterparts in the west. From their standpoint, investment policy is aimed entirely toward increasing the productive power of the nation. That is why China has built more than 20,000 kilometers of high speed rail lines, none of which will produce immediate monetary profit. If the nation is being developed, and if the people are being uplifted, this is not a Risk, from the standpoint of China's leaders. It is a scientifically grounded faith in the future.

Throughout this credit expansion, China has maintained relatively high interest rates, now standing at 7 percent. Compare this to Wall Street institutions, investment banks, hedge funds, vulture funds, equity funds, where investment is computed as to its immediate monetary return, and the speculative frenzy has been financed through interest rates standing near 1 percent.

At the September 4 Hangzhou summit of the G-20 nations, Chinese President Xi Jinping stated, "Facing the current challenges, we can't rely on fiscal and monetary policies. We must envision an all-dimensional, multi-tiered and wide-ranging approach to innovation which is driven by innovation in science and technology, but goes beyond it to cover development philosophy, institutional mechanisms, and business models, so that innovation will be shared by all."

Leverage

A Hamiltonian Credit System *is* a credit system. It utilizes the power of banking to finance useful enterprises which otherwise would lie dormant. The multiplier effect of properly regulated credit is, in one sense, human creativity being deployed to advance the human condition. The problem today is that since the repeal of Glass-Steagall, or going back further, to the policy changes made in the 1970s by Richard Nixon and Jimmy Carter, the true purpose of nationally-directed public credit has been lost. People have become so mentally damaged that speculators, vulture capitalists and asset-strippers who use highly leveraged loans to maximize monetary profits, are oftentimes viewed as financial geniuses through their "creative use" of monetary multipliers.

The same problem is seen in the fad of Public Private Partnerships (PPPs). There is nothing wrong—and it is sometimes very beneficial—to bring private corporations into a partnership with the government on particular projects, under strict government leadership. The reality, however, is that PPPs have primarily functioned as sweetheart deals to secure huge financial windfalls for the companies and investors involved, while also, as in the cases of "privatization" of key public necessities (roads, electricity, water, etc.), resulting in an abandonment by the government of its responsibility to defend the General Welfare, and the imposition of onerous increases in the cost of the related commodities for the citizenry.

People today simply do not understand what Public Credit is.

IV. LaRouche's Four Laws

All of the above cited problems might be avoided and a successful transformation of American policy toward entering into the New Global Paradigm accomplished, through a faithful adherence to the principles defined by Lyndon LaRouche in his "Four Laws." That document is readily available on the Internet. There is no reason to not read it, to not study it, to not discuss it with friends and associates. It is the modern-day Hamiltonian solution to this crisis. Wall Street suffered a devastating defeat in the Presidential election. It is LaRouche's "Four Laws" which now define what the new policy must be. If you haven't studied it, you are simply not competent to speak to what must be done in the United States at this time.

Here, we quote a few short sections.

• Immediate re-enactment of the Glass-Steagall law instituted by U.S. President Franklin D. Roosevelt, without modification, as to principle of action...

FDR Library Photo Collection

President Franklin Roosevelt inspecting the construction of the Boulder Dam, Sept. 30, 1935.

• A return to a system of top-down and thoroughly defined National Banking.... For the present circumstances, all other banking and currency policies, are to be superseded, or, simply, discontinued... Banks qualifying for operations under this provision, shall be assessed for their proven competence to operate as under the national authority for creating and composing the elements of this essential practice, which had been assigned, as by tradition, to the original office of Secretary of the U.S. Treasury under Alexander Hamilton.

• The purpose of the use of a Federal Credit-system, is to generate high-productivity trends in improvements of employment, with the accompanying intention, to increase the physical-economic productivity, and the standard of living of the persons and households of the United States... to create a general economic recovery of the nation, per capita, and for rate of net effects in productivity, and by reliance on the essential human principle, which distinguishes the human personality from the systemic characteristics of the lower forms of life....

NASA

During President John F. Kennedy's visit to the spaceport Nov. 16, 1963, he speaks with George Low (far left), NASA's chief of manned spaceflight, and from Kennedy's left, Mercury astronauts Gordon Cooper and Gus Grissom, and G. Merritt Preston, chief of the Manned Spacecraft Center.

• Adopt a Fusion-Driver 'Crash Program.'

These quotations are brief, and they do not represent—in any way—the full import of what Mr. LaRouche writes. Nevertheless, they give some indication of the change in paradigm which is needed in the United States at this moment.

It is also critical to confront the inescapable reality, that unless the national government acts to shut down the speculative bubble, by enacting Glass-Steagall and returning to national banking methods grounded in the *Reports* of Alexander Hamilton, a wrenching collapse, and all of its accompanying horrors, is a certainty.

Barack Obama and George W. Bush have served the interests of the City of London and Wall Street. Our entire banking and financial system was corrupted, changed from its purpose as defined by Alexander Hamilton and exemplified in the policies of Abraham Lincoln and Franklin Roosevelt. There is no need for the national government to make deals with speculators or to "entice" private investors into participation in rebuilding the nation. The Constitutional Government sets all the rules. It must now lead. China, Russia and many other nations are waiting for America to join the New Paradigm. All that is required from the United States is a return to Hamiltonian principles.

It is also in the concluding section of his "Four Laws," called "Vernadsky On Man & Creation," that Lyndon LaRouche enunciates the most scientifically precise discussion of *Actual Human Productivity* that has been given by anyone up to this moment. It is here that LaRouche defines the actual *Potential* of the human species for developing its creative powers. Any discussion of "productivity" or economic investment policies which does not proceed from the principles therein presented by LaRouche is incompetent and will fail. Read the "Four Laws." Study them.

V. Unifying the Nation

In his *Vindication*, Hamilton writes,

With some men the hardest thing to forgive is the demonstration of their errors,—the manifestation that they are not infallible. Mortified vanity is one of the most corroding emotions of the human mind; one of the most unextinguishable sources of animosity and hatred.

At this moment, the hatred and animosity of which Hamilton speaks, is palpable. The elites of the Democratic and Republican parties are going wild. George Soros is gnashing his teeth. A great deal of confusion and fear is being deliberately spread in the news media. The muckety-mucks of the British Empire and the controllers of the trans-Atlantic financial empire are apoplectic.

Yet, amidst this ongoing warfare and all of the chaos, seemingly paradoxically, this is a moment at which a true sense of national unity might be accomplished within the nation.

Xi Jinping has called his "One Belt-One Road" initiative for global economic development a "Win-Win" policy. Were the majority of Americans to witness, at this moment, a return to a Hamiltonian outlook and policy orientation, unfolding over the coming weeks and months, growing numbers of these same Americans would begin to experience their own "Win-Win" revelation. As with Lincoln's addressing the "better angels of our nature," or Roosevelt with Glass-Steagall and his other great national measures, or John Kennedy with the Apollo Project, a transformation of the psyche and the culture of America becomes possible if certain key steps are taken.

Take the ending of the war confrontation with Russia, the abandonment of the Bush/Obama policy of permanent warfare and the mass killing of civilians, and the start of a rebuilding of the U.S. physical economy. With certain bold actions, the nation begins to heal and to look, hesitantly, with optimism toward the future.

Things now seen as pie-in-the-sky impossibilities become real. Fusion energy. A return to the Moon. The large scale economic development of Mexico, Central America, Africa and other impoverished areas. The revival of Classical Culture. Optimism, a belief in the future, is the key.

This is the future LaRouche defines in his "Four Laws." This is the future made possible through a return to Hamiltonian principles. And this is a future *already present* in the New Paradigm of Xi Jinping, Vladimir Putin, and their friends and collaborators in nations all over the world. Shall we join with them?

III. From Africa

INTEGRATION INTERVIEWS *EIR*'S DAVID CHERRY

What Should Africa Expect From President Trump?

Intégration, *a French-language weekly published in Yaoundé, Cameroon, Central Africa, interviewed David Cherry of* Executive Intelligence Review *in its Nov. 14 issue. The interview, conducted by Celestin Ngoa Balla, is headlined "In rejecting Hillary Clinton, the American people have driven back the threat of nuclear war." It is published here in its English version by permission of* Intégration. *Subheads have been added.*

Intégration: What do you think the peoples of Africa should expect from Donald Trump, who has just won the presidential election in the USA?

David Cherry: In electing Trump, the American people have *rejected* the policies of the elites, of the past 25 years and more. That does not mean that our citizens know, or agree on, what the alternative should be. They do not. They elected Trump, but what does Trump stand for?

What one can say is that, by rejecting Hillary Clinton, the American people have pushed back the threat of nuclear war, at least for the time being. Trump does not regard Russia as the enemy of the United States. This marks him off sharply from the policies of President Obama and Hillary Clinton, who see Russia as an obstacle to their plans to consolidate unipolar world rule. Obama's provocative actions show that he is capable of triggering a thermonuclear World War III in his contest of wills with Russia.

The election of Trump is part of a sea change around the world, initiated by the fortunate combination of Russian President Vladimir Putin and Chinese President Xi Jinping. It means the rejection of policies formerly hegemonic world-wide. We see that change in China's New Silk Road policy, in the creation of the Asian Infrastructure Investment Bank (AIIB) and other new development banks, and in the emergence of the BRICS association of nations. We see it in Germany, in the increasing rejection by German industrial and commercial institutions of Obama's policy of sanctions against doing business with Russia. We see it in the election of Rodrigo Duterte as President of the Philippines. And we

The interview is billed here on the front page, lower left.

see it in the greater independence of South Africa's President Zuma, relative to London and Washington.

Americans Have Work To Do

In the United States, the real work remains to be done—the work of building an understanding among the people of what is needed to bring the human species to a higher level of moral, physical, and cognitive existence. The movement of Lyndon and Helga LaRouche, which I represent as a contributor to *Executive Intelligence Review*, is dedicated to doing just that. Lyndon LaRouche (in his "Four Laws") provides a foundation, by calling for Glass-Steagall separation of commercial banking from speculative banking; establishment of a national bank as Alexander Hamilton defined it; use of a federal credit system to increase employment, productivity, and living standards; and a science driver for the economy in the form of a crash program to develop nuclear fusion as a source of energy.

We must also build an entirely new system of relations among sovereign nations. It must be based on a rejection of artificial and arbitrary divisions of humankind, such as by race or even by competing national interests, in favor of cooperation among all people for the benefit of the entire human race. Such a system must finally do away with war as means of settling issues. We must seek immediately to create such a new system of cooperative effort for human progress on this planet, and beyond, extending man's role in the universe. We seek not only a "new deal" here in the United States, but a global "new deal," as well as what Mr. La-Rouche calls "a new deal for the universe"—the revival of the U.S. Space Program in cooperation with other nations, such as China. This is the only way that we can create a secure peace. It will be a process, taken in steps, but it must be done.

Murder of Gaddafi, Demolition of Libya

Intégration: How do you see Barack Obama's balance sheet with respect to Africa, now that he is at the end of his term?

Cherry: Obama's policy towards Africa has been to deliberately create conditions of managed genocide. This is and has been the policy towards the continent by the British empire and its dying Anglo-American dominated trans-Atlantic financial system. Obama has attempted to block any real economic development, and especially the vitally necessary development of nuclear energy as a major power source, and has otherwise sought to limit the development of high-speed rail transportation corridors and water management plans.

The sum total of his policy is murder, both in the present and for the future. Fortunately, there is an alternative coming from the BRICS nations, especially Russia and China, which is designed to overcome the sabotage of the British and their puppet, Obama, and offer such development. The recent Russian-South African nuclear deal is an example of this policy, which has brought the wrath of Obama down upon the Zuma government.

Intégration: Do you think that Barack Obama could have prevented the fall and assassination of Muammar Gaddafi?

Cherry: Obama orchestrated the overthrow and the murder of Muammar Gadaffi. He is therefore directly responsible for the rise—in the vacuum created by the collapse of Gadaffi's government—of the Islamic State terrorists, and for the slaughter that has ensued. The overthrow of Gaddafi was a part of Obama's scheme to arm large numbers of Islamist terrorists who could eventually pose a threat to the integrity of Russia. That idea went back to Zbigniew Brzezinski. With the disintegration of the Libyan state, Libyan and other weapons were shipped from Libya to Syria through Turkey. While the country was being destroyed, Gaddafi eventually, and reluctantly, agreed to leave the country, and the arrangements were in place. Obama arranged to have him murdered instead. Obama enjoys killing. He was influenced by his step-father, one of the organizers of the massacres of at least a half million Indonesians on behalf of U.S. policy in 1965.

Attack on South Africa To Stop BRICS

Intégration: Right now, Obama is being accused of working to overthrow Jacob Zuma, President of South Africa. How do you explain this?

Cherry: Obama is a puppet of the British Empire, and serves the policy interests of the City of London and its Wall Street satrapy. His target is not President Zuma *per se*, but the sovereign nation of South Africa. By going after Zuma and factions in the ANC which support him, the intention of the people behind Obama is to make South Africa a bloody ungovernable mess, and to prevent it from playing a leadership role on the African continent and globally, in bringing into full existence the new paradigm for which the BRICS alliance is the seed crystal. A state of war already exists between the British imperial faction of the global elites, and the BRICS nations whose leadership is Russia and China. The attack on Zuma should be seen as part of that war, just as the overthrow of President Dilma Rousseff of Brazil was part of it.

The Manipulation of Corruption

Intégration: And how do you answer those who say that the decline in Zuma's power comes from Guptagate, in other words from his inclination to corruption?

Cherry: The Guptas are not the cause of Zuma's problem but a convenient way to conceal what is actually going on. Let us be direct: the entire globalist system is massively corrupt and that corruption has been paid for in the blood of its innocent victims, whose nations have been looted. As long as this system exists—the Empire of Money—then its sleaze will be used to corrupt governments by those who run the system, for their benefit. The Guptas are part of this sleaze and slime, and are so used.

The reason that Zuma has been targeted is not—I repeat not—because of his alleged corruption or cronyism, but because he has walked, with the urging and support of Russian President Putin, through the doorway into a new system represented by the BRICS, taking his nation along with him. This has made London and Wall Street crazy with rage and anger, so they have deployed their "clean government" apparatus, including their agents in the media, to try to reverse the change that Zuma initiated and plunge the nation into chaos.

The pawprints of this British/Obama beast behind the operation are out in the open, even if generally unreported. For example, the so-called Public Protector in South Africa, who has done a great deal of damage to President Zuma's standing, is an officer of state. Yet she had received $500,000 from the U.S. Agency for International Development (USAID), which is guided by the U.S. President, Secretary of State, and National Security Council.[1] That is corruption! The Public Protector's most recent report, called "State of Capture," which attempted to implicate a number of government figures in Guptagate, was written for her by the auditing firm PricewaterhouseCoopers, headquartered in London.

---

1. The Public Protector's allies have clarified that the $500,000 from USAID was actually given to the South African Department of Justice, and only a part of it was eventually earmarked for the Public Protector. In other words, the corruption is much more widespread than initially reported.

South African Broadcasting Corp.

South African President Jacob Zuma's address to 3,000 ANC party cadre in Pietermaritzburg, Nov. 18, on the necessity of the BRICS, was carried live on national television.

The British Role

Intégration: Are there other African countries in Obama's sights? In your opinion, what should be the attitude of the African Union to this threat?

Cherry: Any nation that shows a sign of moving out of control of the British Empire and financial power, in London and Wall Street, is a target. The African Union could play a role in denouncing such operations, but it is itself a victim of manipulations to prevent it from having a decisive voice. The honest press and media need to play a more aggressive role in defending nations from such attacks by the enemies of mankind. Having the kind of dialogue we are having shows the helpful and important role that the press can play—if they have the guts to stand up to the evil and corrupt establishment which effectively censors the truth, denying people access to it. We must, together fight for the truth, no matter what the cost.

Intégration: Does Britain participate in this campaign against South Africa?

Cherry: The British are at the very center of the attack on the sovereign nation of South Africa, using their puppet Obama as their instrumentality. One of South Africa's vulnerabilities is its continued participation in the institutions of that Empire, including the Commonwealth. These institutions serve as channels of corruption, as well as for undermining the policy initiatives that are required for national survival, including nuclear energy development.

The mistake that many people make is to believe the Empire's self-serving propaganda that it has changed, that it has no real power, that the Queen and Royal Family are merely entertainment for the tabloids. This is a lie, and the world is littered with the bodies of people who have opposed its interests, including some among its own, such as Princess Diana. The Queen is an evil, murderous bitch, and Obama kisses her disgusting butt.

Fortunately the winds of the global revolution, of which the Trump election is a part, must eventually sweep the British Empire away. If that does not happen, then mankind will not survive. I share Mr. LaRouche's optimism that the change will be accomplished.

The American People Must Act

Intégration: What lies ahead: a new cold war or third world war?

Cherry: We are already in the early stages of a new global war. Those who speak of a new cold war are either fools or deliberately lying about what must be the consequences of a conflict between the old, dying system and the emerging new paradigm, led by President Putin of Russia and President Xi of China. The two cannot co-exist, and since the Russians and the Chinese recognize that the abandonment of their current efforts means death—the death of their nations and of the rest of the world in the holocaust brought on by the policies of the trans-Atlantic system—they have no interest in, or intention of backing down.

The fight right now is to end the threat of war by creating a new system of relations among nations, based on peace and development, and scientific progress through cooperation. This is the only effective "war avoidance" strategy, and it is what I am committed to, and would urge others to become so committed.

The election of Mr. Trump offers us a potential for creating a great and necessary change in the United States, breaking it away from the British Empire, placing it back on its historic mission as defined by such great American Presidents as Abraham Lincoln, and in the last century Franklin Roosevelt and John Kennedy. It is not so much about what Mr. Trump will do, but about what the American people must do to create the necessary change in policy.

Intégration: Can Donald Trump's arrival at the White House save the skin of Jacob Zuma and in turn the New Cold War?

Cherry: It is important to recognize that the power of the old, dying empire is weakening. In reality, no one need listen to it. It has the power to destroy the whole world, but little else effectively if people choose to resist. If they do so now, and if they rally around the policies for peace and development such as the "One Road, One Belt" program of President Xi and Mr. La-Rouche's "4 Laws," if we can move towards a new co-operative paradigm among nations and peoples, in the interests of all humanity, then we can finally sweep the British Empire and what it represents into the dustbin of history, where it belongs. It won't be easy, but it can be done. It must be done.

South Africa's Zuma Fights for the BRICS

by David Cherry

Nov. 21—South African President Jacob Zuma has just launched a campaign—in his capacity as president of the ruling African National Congress (ANC)—to educate his party's cadre on the crucial role of the BRICS, the world-building movement, in South Africa's future and the future of the world. Zuma began his campaign Nov. 18—he calls it an "unofficial campaign tour"—with an address to 3,000 cadre in Pietermaritzburg, not far from Durban. It was carried live to a national television audience by the South African Broadcasting Corporation, and live to audiences throughout southern Africa by eNews Channel Africa (eNCA). The next day, Zuma brought the message to cadre in KwaDukuza, another town in the area. He is expected to continue these addresses—they are almost tutorials—throughout the country.

Zuma's breakthrough, his decision to take personal responsibility to fight for the BRICS, comes after members of his government, among others—for the past year and more—have taken an interest in the strategic message of Ramasimong Phillip Tsokolibane, leader of La-Rouche South Africa. Tsokolibane has stressed that South Africa is crucial to the BRICS as its initial connection to Africa, and that conversely, South Africa will not thrive, nor even survive, without the economic independence enabled by the BRICS, and its "Build! Build! Build!" spirit. For some, this much was not news.

But, Tsokolibane emphasized, South Africa will be torn out of the BRICS by the hybrid warfare for regime change, coming from the City of London and Wall

Street, unless the South African people are made aware of what BRICS is and what is at stake, and are mobilized in its support. For the vast majority of South Africans, the BRICS is a distant "something," if they have heard of it at all. The South African mass media, steered by the British empire, have kept it that way.

The regime-change operations of U.S. President Obama and his controllers in Buckingham Palace have generated a rising tide of confusion and misdirection, even among ANC members. The regime-change propaganda, and the agitation of many thousands of agents of influence, leaves many South Africans thinking that if President Zuma would just resign, it would be the first step toward solving South Africa's problems. The opposite is true: Strengthening the BRICS is that necessary first step.

Zuma's Message

In his addresses, Zuma delivered this message:

The BRICS is a powerful combination in the world's balance of forces and it thinks independently [of the trans-Atlantic consensus]. BRICS members Russia and China are permanent members of the UN Security Council with veto power. China is the number one economic power in the world. BRICS has interfered with the global balance of forces, posing a serious threat to other powerful forces. The relationship among the BRICS countries is growing. Political power without control of the economy does not mean anything; we need the BRICS and its program to gain control over our own economy. That is why South Africa [under Zuma] was the one that pushed for the BRICS bank.

Zuma emphasized that South Africa's membership in the BRICS was *the* reason for the relentless attacks on him, which, he correctly pointed out, were really attacks on South Africa.

The regime-changers do not want an open, public debate on the BRICS, free of disinformation. They would lose. Instead, they create a sequence of soap operas around President Zuma, to destroy the President who has worked to make the BRICS a reality. Meanwhile, the BRICS is not brought into public discussion. Zuma is now scuppering that game by making BRICS the issue.

Referring to these soap operas, Zuma said, "If you look at what's happening in South Africa today, you'd swear we're quarrelling among ourselves, and not see the hand that is influencing it all."

He pointed to the impeachment of Brazilian President Dilma Rousseff in August as an attack on BRICS. And they have tried that here, he said. "Here in South Africa, we've been to Parliament seven times with a vote of no confidence."

The no confidence votes do not pass, but they have been successful as psychological warfare, eroding confidence and ANC solidarity, and sowing confusion.

Zuma also recalled what happened in December 2015, when he attempted to replace his finance minister with one who would be responsive to a truly South African and BRICS agenda:

You do everything according to the Constitution, and then people that control the economy tell you to drop everything; they want to burn the country, and you can see that if you don't change your decision, they *will* really burn the country.

The ratings agencies "are part of the arsenal being used by countries seeking to smash the BRICS alliance," Zuma said.

The agencies are in South Africa right now. Moody's, Fitch, and S&P are sniffing around and are expected to lower the country's ratings before the end of the year.

Zuma pointed to an example of the regime-changers' disinformation: "China is growing faster than all other countries, but they're always saying 'that economy is sluggish.' All because they're just fighting BRICS."

A Window of Opportunity

Zuma spoke eloquently for 70 minutes to attentive audiences that listened as he spoke and sang when he sang. Many of his hearers wore t-shirts printed with the message, "Hands Off My President."

A pastor in Pretoria who watched one of the broadcasts, concluded, "The BRICS revolution as an economic revolution is a global *force* in South Africa's favor, but we are too clouded by petty politics to see it."

Zuma recently declared, "I am not afraid of jail." He recognizes that he, personally, must continue this fight as long as it takes, even if he is out of office.

With the defeat of President Obama's intended successor, Hillary Clinton, and the election of an anti-establishment President—or more precisely, one who rejects the London-Wall Street outlook at least for now—there is a valuable window of opportunity that South African patriots must not miss.

dacherry3@yahoo.com

Trump Swept in by Global Wave Against Old Order of War and Collapse

by Ramasimong Phillip Tsokolibane, leader of LaRouche South Africa

Nov. 13—On behalf of the La-Rouche movement in South Africa, I offer my congratulations to President-elect Donald Trump on his victory over the corrupt Anglo-American elite and its policy of economic collapse and war. I join President Jacob Zuma in wishing the new American President success. I hope that Mr. Trump and his administration are able to bring the United States into a new era of cooperation with my nation. I hope he and his administration will seek peaceful economic development with all nations, and avoid war.

Ramasimong Phillip Tsokolibane

But let us be clear about what happened on November 8 and what must happen if we are indeed to secure peace and development for all mankind.

President-elect Trump comes into office riding a global wave of revulsion and rejection, by people all around the globe, now including the citizens of the United States—rejection of the failed policies of the global elites. Those policies have led to the collapse of the elites' trans-Atlantic empire of money, delivering us to the brink of general thermonuclear war with Russia and China—the elites' last remaining option. It was those policies—of the current U.S. President, Barack Obama, and his clone Hillary Clinton—that the American people rejected Tuesday in a solid vote.

Mr. Trump had skillfully positioned himself to be the beneficiary of this rejection of the Obama-Hillary Clinton program of war and economic collapse. Repeatedly, he repudiated the policy of confrontation against Russian President Putin and expressed his support for reinstating the Glass-Steagall legislation of 1933, the repeal of which by Bill Clinton in 1999, unleashed the wild speculative orgy by Wall Street that is still ongoing. Just as Britons—defying the 'advice' of the elite and its lying media and pollsters—rebelled by voting to leave the failed European Union, forcing the so-called Brexit, so have American voters overturned the applecart, crushing Clinton, who was heavily favored by Wall Street, the media, pollsters, and pundits.

But as the world's leading economist, American statesman Lyndon LaRouche, tells us in his response to the election of Mr. Trump, this has only bought us a temporary respite from the drive towards war by Obama. There is no secure and stable global system among nations at this point that can secure peace. Unless such a system is built, we will soon, once again, be back on a path towards war.

We can see the outlines of such a new system in the way the BRICS alliance (Brazil, Russia, India, China, South Africa) functions, in which South Africa plays a crucial role. The BRICS seek a common ground for cooperative efforts, realizing that peace and prosperity come with the betterment of all, at the expense of none. This is in complete defiance of the globalist, monetarist system in which the benefit of a few oligarchical interests comes at the expense of everyone else.

At root there are two distinct views of humanity. The current, dying system sees man as merely a more capable beast, whose animal urges and interests are curbed by the laws of competition.

But men are not animals! We are uniquely creative beings who, through our creativity, can alter the course of our own history. It is our creativity that makes us master of our vast universe and of our future in it.

Mr. LaRouche warns us that it has now become an urgent matter that we bring relations among nations and peoples into agreement with this human view of man as a creative, sentient being. To do so we must, once and for all, do away with the systems of competition among men and nations, including geopolitics itself. Our new paradigm's sole principle is to nurture the increase in the creative potential of mankind as whole, and of each individual human being. Such a system has no place for war as a means for settling disputes among na-

PIB India

Leaders of the BRICS nations in Goa, India for the annual BRICS Summit, Oct. 16, 2016. In front (left to right) are Xi Jinping (China), Narendra Modi (India), and Vladimir Putin (Russia). Behind Putin are Jacob Zuma (South Africa) and Michel Temer (Brazil).

tions—an urgent necessity—as we now possess weapons that can destroy us all.

We will bring about this new system in steps of cooperative development, such as by participating in Chinese President Xi Jinping's win-win strategy of development called One Belt, One Road, which is building infrastructure projects and development corridors throughout Eurasia and into Africa. The One Belt, One Road project (the New Silk Road), when extended to the whole world, is a plan identical to the World Land-Bridge proposal that Mr. LaRouche and his wife Helga Zepp-LaRouche have championed for more than 30 years.

The new system will also require increased cooperation in our exploration of space as a global mission for mankind, and in a crash program for the development of thermonuclear fusion as the new energy platform—of much higher energy-flux density—for our booming global economy.

Mr. LaRouche has insisted on the adoption of Alexander Hamilton's approach in creating the new, global economic system, and has set out the necessary principles in his 'Four Laws,' as follows:

1. Protect banks from speculation. Return to a strict separation between commercial and investment (speculative) banking, and protect the legitimate functions of commercial banking, by enacting laws that are identical in purpose and content to Franklin Roosevelt's Glass-Steagall legislation.

2. Hamiltonian systems of national banking. Create or return to a Hamiltonian system of national banking, and create National Banks, to replace the current monetarist system of private central banking.

3. Government credit to increase productive employment. Provide government credit to increase the quality and quantity of productive work, measured in increases in the productive powers of labor and in energy-flux density.

4. Fusion power and space programs. Use national resources to launch a worldwide crash program or programs to master and widely deploy fusion power and related technologies, and to build up full-spectrum space programs.

For a fuller exposition of LaRouche's Four Laws, go to: http://action.larouchepac.com/know_the_full_story

These are the principles that must define the policy of a new Trump administration. But we must not rely on Mr. Trump to put them on the agenda. It is the responsibility of all men and women of vision and courage in all nations around the world to take personal responsibility for bringing into being the new, just world order and to move on the potential opened up by the great rejection and change that took place in the United States this week. I pledge my full devotion and effort to that task.

ramasimongt@hotmail.com

Bush and Obama War Crimes Exposed—President-Elect Trump Should Agree

Nov. 22 (EIRNS)—The following statement, by Republican Senator Richard H. Black of the Virginia Senate, came in response to a warning from Rep. Ted Lieu (D-CA) that U.S. support and collaboration with Saudi Arabia in the criminal war against Yemen was putting US military personnel at risk of prosecution for war crimes. Sen. Black was the former Chief of the Criminal Law Division in the Office of the Judge Advocate General at the Pentagon.

"I agree with Rep. Lieu's legal analysis. However, I believe the more practical aspect of this is the legal exposure of our most senior officials, who directed our servicemen's actions. Under the precedent set by the American War Crimes Tribunal of Japanese General Yamashita following WWII, the senior commander is criminally liable for generalized criminal misconduct by his subordinates. This applies to conduct of which he knew or should have known.

"America has widely flouted international norms of conduct in its wars of aggression against Serbia, Iraq, Libya, Syria, and now Yemen. Some acts appear to constitute common law crimes—such as our refusal to accept the surrender of Col. Kaddafi when he offered to leave Libya. The U.S., Great Britain, and France reportedly conferred before deciding to ignore his offer to abdicate, and facilitated his murder instead.

"By flouting settled norms of wartime conduct, the U.S. has severely undermined its moral authority and diminished its power across the globe. While I support a robust defense, we gain nothing by fighting wars to advance globalism—particularly when such wars violate the Law of Land Warfare."

www.ingramcontent.com/pod-product-compliance
Lightning Source LLC
Chambersburg PA
CBHW051951280526
45789CB00009B/3249